101 THINGS THAT PLAY IN PEORIA

101 Things That Play In Peoria is a publication of the *Journal Star*

101 Things That Play In Peoria

ISBN-13: 978-1512060041

JournalStar | pjstar.com

Book published by the *Journal Star*
1 News Plaza
Peoria, IL 61643
www.pjstar.com

Publisher: Ken Mauser
Executive Editor: Dennis Anderson
Managing Editor: Sally McKee
Human Resources Director: Michelle Ferguson
Consumer Sales and Marketing Director: Norb Gray
Marketing and Public Affairs Manager: Phil Jordan
Controller: Brian Kier
Senior Director of Production: Mike Kreppert
Advertising Director: Dave Lammers
Information Systems Manager: Ron Rude
Main 101 Things That Play In Peoria Writer: Phil Luciano
Main Book Designer: Chris Grimm

101 THINGS THAT PLAY IN PEORIA CONTENTS

101 Things' vibe plays into Peoria's Spirit

You know how sports teams have an extra teammate?

In football, the concept is known as "The 12th Man." The title refers to die-hard supporters who stay loyal through thick and thin.

We have something like that with our lengthy project, 101 Things That Play in Peoria.

But here, I'd like to add one more. Call it the 102nd Thing: The Peoria Spirit.

What is that? It's feisty, it's gritty, it's steadfast.

What is it not? Flashy, trendy or flighty.

Granted, that's not a comprehensive definition. The framing is wide, kind of like the criteria for 101 Things — which from the outset sought to describe the uniqueness of Peoria as a sum of its distinctive parts.

What does that have to do with the Peoria Spirit? Many of you were kind enough to share suggestions, some of which didn't make the final list. Some weren't things, some were obscure,

PHIL
LUCIANO

5

some just didn't fit.

Usually, readers don't like to hear "no" from their newspaper. I understand that, because it often happens to me.

But with readers, even if the answer is valid and polite, they won't accept a "no, thank you." Usually, they rant that I'm unfair and that I'm a stupid doody-head. Or something like that.

Yet with 101 Things, the responses were taken as challenges. Readers almost always said, "Oh, I get where you're coming from. Then how about this suggestion? Or maybe do you know about this thing?"

It was weird, as if we were all adults — even, shockingly, me — and working together on something. Granted, it's not as if 101 Things will cure diseases or end poverty. Still, the project was remarkable for the positive vibe. Reader or writer, it's nice to par-

take in something like that.

Times like those, I started thinking of the Peoria Spirit. This town isn't perfect, but I see brokenness as endearing. Still, some locals demean Peoria for not being trendy and polished enough to suit their tastes. These are likely the type of insufferable, yammering posers willing to shell out tall cash for a purebred, unblemished hound that sits still and quiet all day. I prefer a snarling, mottled mutt with bad breath and a lazy eye — harder to love, perhaps, but less maintenance and more character.

Peoria oozes character, bad and good — and that's part of the Peoria Spirit. Hereabouts, despite plenty of individual differences, we tend to share one trait: compassion. I've lived on both coasts and a few burgs in between, yet I've never seen a place with more charities and fundraisers, from national

efforts to spaghetti dinners.

Peoria — a tough town with a soft heart — is generous with money and time, yet without doing a lot of bragging. That's something to be proud of.

And I hope you're proud of 101 Things. It involved a lot of hard work at 1 News Plaza. Teressa Hargrove put the photos together, while Matt Dayhoff handled videos. In both cases, they usually had nothing to use but my lackluster camera work, which they had to transform into something decent.

Meanwhile, the project leaned on efforts from writers Steve Tarter, Chris Kaergard, Kirk Wessler and Pam Adams, plus photographers David Zalaznik and Ron Johnson. Thanks to all.

PHIL LUCIANO is a Journal Star columnist. He can be reached at pluciano@pjstar.com, facebook.com/philluciano or (309)686-3155.

At 17.5 feet tall, you can't miss Vanna Whitewall

She's the perfect woman times three, measuring 108-72-107, as flaunted every summer in a red bikini. In colder months, she often sports a more modest skirt-pullover combo, though — at 17½ feet tall and weighing 450 pounds of pure fiberglass — she always commands attention.

With her left arm thrown up, she might look like a hitchhiker. Actually, that arm once held a tire, back in the 1960s when she was born as Miss Uniroyal, one of that company's three mascots. She first appeared at Peoria Plaza Tire, 1800 SW Washington St., at its grand opening in 1968.

After a makeover in 1988, she got her permanent

101 THINGS THAT PLAY IN PEORIA

nickname: Vanna Whitewall.

She's not just a head-turner but one tough dame. In 2005, a wayward car plowed into Vanna, fracturing her right foot and left leg — and, worrisome for any fashion-conscious gal, damaging a high heel. After repairs at an auto shop, she was back at her familiar post in front of the shop.

And as a Peoria landmark, Vanna Whitewall might be the all-time most valuable employee at Peoria Plaza Tire.

To give directions, workers there long have told callers, "You can't miss us. Just look for the 17½-foot-tall gal outside."

CLUE FOR NEXT ITEM: Follow your nose to this tasty treasure.

Peorians are drawn to where the nose glows: Emo's

Just like Santa Claus needs Rudolph's red nose for guidance, Peoria depends on the Emo's Dairy Mart clown head.

Need to meet someone in Peoria at a place everyone knows? Just say, "I'll meet you in the Emo's parking lot — you know, the place with the clown." Or, need directions but don't have a GPS? Call someone and ask, "I'm at the Emo's clown. Where do I go from there?"

The landmark consists simply of painted plywood and a light-up nose. But its high profile mixes two key qualities: a central location — Prospect Road and War Memorial Drive — and 50-plus years of history.

101 THINGS THAT PLAY IN PEORIA

Elmer and Marge Harms bought the stand in 1960. Since childhood, he'd been called Emo — no one is sure why — so the couple opted for that name for the business. In 1963, he and his kin came up with the giant clown head as an attention-getter.

Storms have knocked down the clown, but not out. The last facelift occurred in 2011, when current owner Robert Smith replaced most of the head.

Every spring and summer (Emo's is closed otherwise), the nose beckons fans of ice cream and coney dogs, many eager to take photos of Peoria's most famous clown.

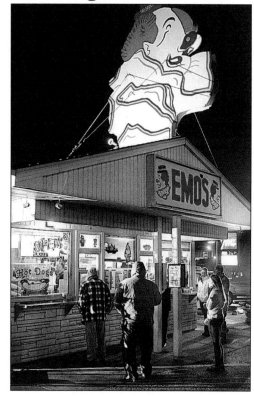

CLUE FOR NEXT ITEM: East of the river, this icon is worth crowing about.

Dignified bird rules the roost at Carl's Bakery

Why did the chicken cross the state? To get to East Peoria.

Carl's Bakery & Cafe, 819 E. Camp St. in East Peoria, has been cranking out pastries, tenderloins and other delights for more than a half-century. But motorists know it best for the top-hatted rooster out front.

Several decades ago, the Weber family spotted a 20-foot fowl at a restaurant show in Chicago. They decided it to make room for the massive bird outside the eatery. So, by trailer, they hauled it down to East Peoria. Years later, owner Edna Weber (who died at age 84 in 2014) often would recall road-tripping with the rooster, which grabbed the attention of behind-the-wheel gawkers.

"Everybody turned and looked like, 'What's that chicken doing going down the road?'" she'd say, chuckling. "Best advertisement we ever did."

The most distinct part of the concrete clucker is his hat, which once was the target of an elaborate prank. A group of high school students swiped the hat and hid it for almost three years, before one of them returned it.

Thank goodness. A giant rooster wouldn't look dignified without proper headwear.

101 THINGS THAT PLAY IN PEORIA

CLUE FOR NEXT ITEM: There's something fishy about this nasty Peoria critter.

Big 'n' bony, Asian carp jump for joy, but few folk are fans

Asian carp have become as much an Illinois River icon as the Par-A-Dice casino and the Spirit of Peoria.

The difference is, nobody likes Asian carp.

In the 1970s, the beastly fish were imported from Asia to fish farms in the South, mostly to help clean commercial ponds. But soon the carp slipped into the Mississippi River basin, where they have proliferated for four decades.

The hearty eaters spawn year-round, often growing 40 inches long and weighing 500 pounds, with some weighing twice that. Aquatic life is 60 percent Asian carp in some sections of the Illinois River.

Conservationists worry about the impact of Asian carp chomping through the underwater food supply. Boaters and skiers have to be wary of the fish, which when spooked by vibrating motors can soar 10 feet up into the air. Often, they'll land with a plop in boats, splattering blood and slime.

Incessant spawning has pushed them from novelty to nuisance. Peoria County is trying to site a private fish-processing plant somewhere in central Illinois, to give anglers a greater, easier incentive to harvest the disgusting fish.

101 THINGS THAT PLAY IN PEORIA

CLUE FOR NEXT ITEM: Though these things aren't pretty, they look down on others.

Grotesque or inspiring, Bradley gargoyles stand out

Since the early days of Bradley University, gargoyles have been a fixture amid campus architecture.

There are four gargoyle statues: two on Bradley Hall and two on the Hayden-Clark Alumni Center. Not to split hairs, but by definition, a gargoyle features a spout through the mouth to spray water away from the side of a building, whereas a grotesque — like The Thinker, which watches over Bradley's west side of campus and sits atop the alumni center — does not have a spout.

Other colleges have gargoyles, but none other boasts one as a mascot. Kaboom! — unveiled in early 2014 — was mod-

eled after The Thinker. The choice was made after the school collected more than 3,200 survey responses that showed the gargoyle beating out the two other options: lion and eagle. According to a university press release at the time of the announcement of the mascot, "The descriptor (Kaboom!) can be used to emphasize the success of all Bradley University students and their wide-ranging activities of excellence."

The private university had been without an actual mascot since 2000, when it officially rid itself of the bobcat. The Braves, Bradley's nickname since the 1920s, remains.

CLUE FOR NEXT ITEM:
Big voice, big belly, big stature.

11

Ingersoll statue a lasting tribute to Peoria orator, attorney

Looking out over Glen Oak Park is a statue of a man who's been referred to as "the best-known American of the post-Civil War period."

Robert Green Ingersoll got that reputation as an orator, traveling about the country, giving speeches on philosophy, religion and history.

Described as a free thinker, Ingersoll also was known as "Peoria's Pagan Politician" and "The Great Agnostic" for his views on organized religion, which he heartily disapproved of.

An attorney who lived in Peoria from 1858 to 1877, Ingersoll became the state's first attorney general in 1867. His refusal to tone down his religious views probably prevented him from holding high office, but his speaking ability made him a political asset for others.

Ingersoll died in 1899 at the age of 65.

Dedicated in 1911, the Glen Oak statue was produced by Fritz Triebel, who also created the soldiers monument at the Peoria County Courthouse.

101 THINGS THAT PLAY IN PEORIA

CLUE FOR NEXT ITEM: Timber! A basketball player would love to have limbs this long.

'Sentinel of the Bluff' an ancient arboreal wonder

It's hard to imagine everything Peoria's big bur oak has seen since its sapling days.

The lone occupant of Giant Oak Park, on High Street, the tree is said to be at least 300 years old. However, some experts believe it's been there since Columbus discovered the New World, pegging its age at greater than 500 years.

To be sure, it's long been a beloved arboreal landmark. It was mentioned in 1750s surveys by European settlers. Peoria Park District records first indicate efforts to preserve the tree in the mid-1800s.

The natural wonder — long ago dubbed "The Sentinel of the Bluff" — boasts a spread of more than 100 feet. It stands 50 feet tall, with a trunk swelling to the circumference of nearly 30 feet.

Giant Oak Park was dedicated Sept. 5, 1971. The park district has gone to great lengths to protect the tree, including demolishing a nearby building and installing lightning protection.

The tree's fans had a scare in 2014, when winds of up to 60 mph destroyed nearly 30 percent of the oak. But with park district work, the tree again appears sturdy.

For how long? Bur oaks are said to live to 400 years, but most do not get the care of Peoria's big boy. Plus, it's hard to tell if the tree is in middle age or old age. Until the tree falls and its rings are counted, no one can state a definitive age.

101 THINGS THAT PLAY IN PEORIA

CLUE FOR NEXT ITEM: Feline flavor to pizza.

Tiger Sauce has just the right bite for Agatucci's pizza

Under the stewardship of four generations of family, the Italian eatery at 2607 N. University St. has been a stalwart since 1926. But its signature Tiger Sauce didn't debut until 30 years later.

At the time, second-generation owner Frank Agatucci would see Geno Fulgenzi come in most days to order a small, sausage pizza and side salad. Fulgenzi would chomp away at the lettuce, and dip his pizza slices into the leftover tangy, garlicky dressing. He'd often point to the dressing and say, "Frank, you need to put this on the tables. It's fantastic with pizza."

Eventually, Agatucci decided to give it a try, but needed bottles. He wandered around a restaurant-supply store and found some perfect squeeze bottles — though emblazoned with the face of a Bengal tiger and imprinted "tiger sauce." Still, the price had been discounted, so he snapped up a bunch of the odd bottles.

The bottles, placed atop the bar and at tables, became a hit — and the dressing became known as Tiger Sauce. Patrons even began to buy the sauce for home use, and still do today. Though the original bottles long ago vanished, you'll still find Tiger Sauce atop each table at Agatucci's.

101 THINGS THAT PLAY IN PEORIA

CLUE FOR NEXT ITEM: Don't lick this giant cone.

East Peoria enjoys twist on summer treat

The building beckons like a delicious beacon: an oversized ice-cream cone promising delights — frosty and otherwise. M&M Twistee Treat, 1207 E. Washington St. in East Peoria, is shaped like a large cone topped with swirled vanilla ice cream.

The structure is of Florida design. A fellow named Robert "Skip" Skinner built the first Twistee Treat in North Fort Myers, Fla., in 1982. Others would follow, about 90 in all, each nearly 30 feet tall. The company has had ups and downs, with about half of the original buildings demolished.

In 1993, an East Peoria couple spotted a Twistee Treat building for sale in Florida for $25,000 — and snapped it up. Several trucks transported the 24-by-12-foot building to East Peoria, and workers pieced it together in three days.

After more than 20 years, the business (open March through October) continues to beckon drivers, with a menu that includes hot dogs, snacks — and, of course, ice cream.

101 THINGS THAT PLAY IN PEORIA

CLUE FOR NEXT ITEM: Short and stern, she loves school but never comes in for class.

Lydia stands strong in middle of Bradley University campus

It is fitting that Lydia Moss Bradley stands in the middle of the campus that bears her name, on a firm foundation.

After all, without her vision and perseverance, there would be no Bradley University.

In 1997, the school's 101st Founder's Day saw the dedication of the life-size statue on the quad. The bronze likeness — just over 5 feet tall — weighs more than 500 pounds and stands on a granite base.

Bradley was 50 when her husband died of injuries sustained in the overturn of his carriage, in 1867. She already had buried all six of her children, the youngest at 7 months, the oldest at 14 years.

She parlayed her late husband's real-estate fortune into farm development and civic philanthropy. Her public efforts included Laura Bradley Park (named after a daughter), an opera house, a church and a hospital (one briefly known as Bradley Hospital, later known as OSF Saint Francis Medical Center).

But her biggest contribution would be Bradley Polytechnic Institute, which opened Oct. 4, 1897. Not only was it debt free when it opened in October 1897, but Lydia Moss Bradley provided endowment for future development through her $2.8 million estate.

101 THINGS THAT PLAY IN PEORIA

CLUE FOR NEXT ITEM: A parade highlight, his appearance here will be 10 months early.

Taking national pride in first 'Toytown Express'

At the annual Santa Claus Parade, the best float waits for last.

It's the oldest such parade in the nation. According to some tenuous accounts, St. Nick appeared at a parade on Dec. 6, 1887. Actually, that event was a procession of boats and derricks that came down the river from Chillicothe to mark the impending building of a new bridge. And no newspaper stories marked any arrival of a fat man in a red suit.

For sure, though, Santa had begun an annual Peoria pilgrimage by 1895, when newspaper ads touted his arrival at various stores. For Schipper &

![101 THINGS THAT PLAY IN PEORIA]

Block (later Block & Kuhl), the "Toytown Express" locomotive engine roared into the Rock Island Depot, from which a police-escorted, horse-drawn carriage would deliver Santa to the retailer — a mini-parade attended by masses of children and shoppers.

In 1923, the stores extended an open invitation for new floats. In 1950, the parade featured six tiny, live reindeer riding on Santa's float. In 1995, a more permanent float was made, with nine non-live reindeer (including Rudolph at the lead). From his sleigh, a very live Santa waves to the crowd, heralding the arrival of yuletide.

CLUE FOR NEXT ITEM: Where to lunch in nice weather?

Eats on the streets keep workers entertained, invigorated

Different towns sport different signs of spring.

Swallows return to San Juan Capistrano. Cherry trees famously bloom in Washington, D.C. And losing baseball (usually) resumes on the North Side of Chicago.

But in Peoria, spring means food carts Downtown.

Tacos, gyros, egg rolls, teriyaki barbecue chicken, crab rangoon, sweet and sour chicken, lemon shake-ups, tamales, fajitas, wontons, burritos and, of course, tamales and grilled pork chop sandwiches.

Sure, you can step outside just about anywhere and jam a sandwich into your craw. But it's not the same as the Main-Adams noontime fun fest.

Besides eats on the cheap, nice weather offers a respite from the weekday grind. Fannies — secretaries, laborers, junior executives, courthouse workers, visitors — stretch across the concrete berms in and around the courthouse, giving Peoria an uptempo vibe at midday. The communal gathering almost feels like a weekend festival, especially if a middle school band or community-theater troupe is belting out tunes.

Yeah, you'll have to go back to work eventually. But the drudgery seems less dreary after a little invigorating zest, thanks to the food carts.

101 THINGS THAT PLAY IN PEORIA

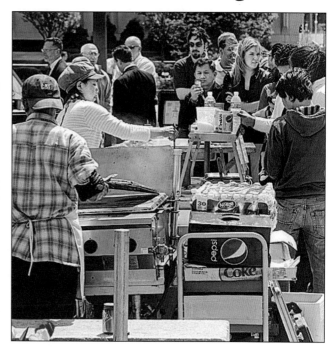

CLUE FOR NEXT ITEM: Saucy artwork almost got axed.

'Nymphs and Satyr' at Richard's on Main

In 1890, Pete Weast bought a risque painting that became a Peoria treasure, but not for the reasons he'd envisioned.

The tavern-keeper apparently knew booze better than art. He shelled out a princely $4,000 for what turned out to be a knock-off of the original "Nymphs and Satyr." (The original, by the acclaimed French painter William-Adophe Bouguereau, now hangs in the renowned Clark Art Institute in Williamstown, Mass.)

The clueless Weast proudly put the forgery inside his Golden Palace Saloon on Jefferson Avenue. The 8-by-10-foot forgery depicts four wood nymphs dragging a leering satyr. In 1901, anti-alcohol crusader Carrie Nation stormed to Peoria, threatening to take her ax to the painting and the rest of the place. But Weast slipped Nation a $50 bribe to get her to leave town.

Weast retired in 1908 and put the painting in storage. The work went ignored until 1970, when it was found just before the old tavern was razed. In 1972, the painting was displayed at the Creve Coeur Club, where it remained until the club was remodeled in the late 1980s. It now is on exhibit at Richard's on Main, 311 Main St. The nymphs and satyr still are grinning, survivors — though fakeries — in Peoria after all these years.

101 THINGS THAT PLAY IN PEORIA

CLUE FOR NEXT ITEM: On this, brothers rolled on as manufacturing pioneers but today get little credit.

Central Illinois natives made automotive history

How key were Charles and Frank Duryea as auto pioneers? None other than Henry Ford said, "The Duryea car was a masterpiece. It did more to start the automobile industry than any other car ever made."

Along the way, the brothers earned credit — if not notoriety — as the first U.S. manufacturer to produce, advertise and sell gasoline-powered cars.

Charles Duryea (born in 1861 near Canton) and Frank (born in 1869 outside Washburn) were bicycle manufacturers in Peoria when they headed east to continue their craft. On Sept. 20, 1893, after researching the internal combustion engine, they first drove the Duryea Motor Wagon, in Springfield, Mass.

A brotherly rift prompted Charles to return to Peoria. In 1898, he created the three-wheeled Duryea Motor Trap in the barn behind his home on Barker Street. The driver was to use a single handle to steer the vehicle, shift gears and throttle the engine. Charles hoped to crank out 100 cars a year but built just a few before running out of money.

In 1901, the original Trap was sold to a Pennsylvania man. It was found there in 1988. A "Bring Home the Duryea" campaign raised $125,000 to buy the car and return it to Peoria.

After several detours while on display, the Duryea Motor Trap is now permanently parked at the Peoria Riverfront Museum.

101 THINGS THAT PLAY IN PEORIA

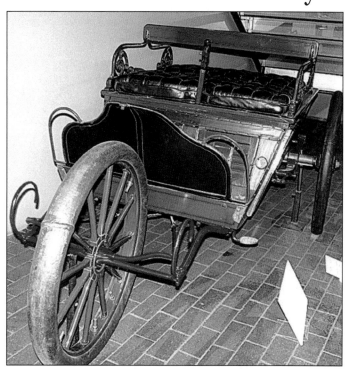

CLUE FOR NEXT ITEM:
Yummiest yellow in town.

Mysterious spread makes Patio Inn the 'cheesiest place in town'

Forever, it seems, the faithful have tried to figure out the secret behind the cheese spread at Castle's Patio Inn.

Whatever is in the mix — Garlic? Oh, yeah. Horseradish? Maybe a touch — the blend serves as the centerpiece of the self-proclaimed "Cheesiest Place in Town" at 802 W. Loucks Ave.

The squat structure, built in 1920 as a grocery, hosted multiple bars after Prohibition, most famously Ray's Patio Inn. Owner Ray Eskridge, who ran the place for 20-some years starting in the 1960s, first brought in the famous cheese spread — no one knows the origin — served free at the bar with crackers. He also coined the term "Patio Inn," apparently because his next-door house had a patio where sometimes he'd move the parties. That tradition ended when he sold the business in the late 1980s, leaving newcomers to this day invariably and unsuccessfully peering around the pub for a patio.

After other ownerships, it was bought in 1993 by Chuck and Barb Castle. They still own the joint, which as always relies heavily on equal parts of warmth, familiarity and nostalgia — and every Christmastime sells more than 4,000 pounds of cheese spread.

101 THINGS THAT PLAY IN PEORIA

CLUE FOR NEXT ITEM:
A president came to see it in 1899.

Soldiers and Sailors Monument commands respect

Perhaps no Peoria landmark commands the solemn respect of the Soldiers and Sailors Monument in the Courthouse Plaza.

Since its 1899 unveiling, the Civil War tribute has demanded visual attention, with its 60-foot column and larger-than-life bronze female figure, arm upraised to inscribe the words "We write on page of granite what they wrought on field of battle."

In 1892, with Civil War patriotism apparently waning, the Ladies Memorial Day Association spearheaded a $40,000 fundraising drive for a war memorial. The monument, titled "Defense of the Flag," was the work of Frederick E. "Fritz" Triebel, who grew up in Peoria, studied sculpture in Italy and became world renowned.

On Oct. 6, 1899, about 70,000 onlookers overflowed the courthouse square for the dedication. President McKinley, accompanied by his wife and most of his Cabinet, told the throng, "This monument awakens sacred memories, fellow citizens, and that is its purpose.

"It was erected ... that it might for all time perpetuate a glorious page of American history. It tells the whole story of war, the siege, the march, bivouac, battle line, the suffering, sacrifices of the brave men, who from '61 to '65 upheld the flag."

101 THINGS THAT PLAY IN PEORIA

CLUE FOR NEXT ITEM: Stretching high into the sky, from earth to heaven — times two.

Rising 230 feet, St. Mary's twin spires are skyline fixture

No element of the Peoria skyline has lingered as long as the twin spires of St. Mary's Cathedral.

Since 1889, the limestone spires, topped with crosses, soar skyward 230 feet, as if reaching for heaven.

The magnificent church, 607 NE Madison Ave., boasts delicately curved arches and flutings. The finished edifice, which cost $110,000, was dedicated by the first Roman Catholic bishop of Peoria, John Lancaster Spalding. He modeled the building after St. Patrick's Cathedral in New York, where he had been ordained a bishop in 1877.

The spires have seen celebrities pass below. Archbishop Fulton Sheen grew up in the parish and attended Spalding Academy before attaining fame as the nation's first televangelist. The famed Von Trapp family sang at the cathedral in one of their first American performances after escaping Austria during World War II. And Mother Teresa visited the cathedral twice.

Today, a motorist westbound on Interstate 74, especially at night, can easily spot the double spires — an image of a church grounded in this world while seemingly stretching toward the next.

101 THINGS THAT PLAY IN PEORIA

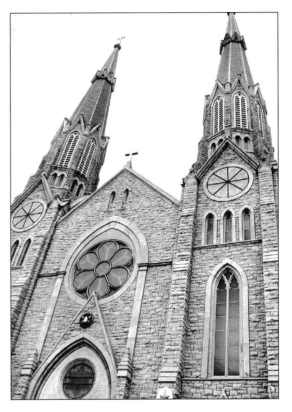

CLUE FOR NEXT ITEM: A car that can fly?
In West Peoria, the future is now.

A car, and arch, in the sky on Farmington Road

For decades, an airborne auto has overlooked Farmington Road, thanks to Neal Auto Parts.

Harry Neal, who started the business 60-some years ago, decided to advertise the place from the sky — with a Cadillac Seville mounted on a pole. In 1986, the enterprise moved a ways down the road, to the current location at 3407 W. Farmington Road. Bob Neal, son of the original owner, wanted a new spin on the sign. He found inspiration from metal workers doing an on-site project. They told him about salvaging a 50-foot arch from a grocery store. Bingo!

The workers sank the arch into a solid 15 yards of concrete and constructed a platform in the middle, 30 feet off the ground. Neal's found a 1982 Buick Regal, nearly useless because of a fire-damaged interior. After the name of the business was painted on each door, the car was hoisted to the platform and secured with four heavy bolts.

The Buick remained up there for nearly three decades, with only birds for company. In 2014, Neal's had to rehab the arch, and in the process took down the car by crane. The vehicle had rusted thoroughly, to the point a replacement was needed.

The Buick went to a salvage yard. A 2006 Infiniti G35 now rests on the arch.

101 THINGS THAT PLAY IN PEORIA

CLUE FOR NEXT ITEM: Many conventioneers have an eye out for this.

The arch at Neal Auto Parts Inc.

World Famous Big Al's a fixture since 1973

For five decades, one particular Downtown sign has beckoned conventioneers, visitors, bachelor parties and other oglers:

"World Famous Big Al's."

The striptease parlor has been a mainstay of the Peoria nightlife scene since 1973. Ask outsiders what they know about Peoria, and chances are they'll name two businesses: Caterpillar Inc. and Big Al's.

The bright neon sign serves as a beacon for fans of exotic dancing, an exclamation point to Peoria's offerings as a convention town. In 1974, the city adopted strict local adult-entertainment regulations that preclude strip bars Downtown. However, by opening a year earlier, Big Al's

was grandfathered as an exception. The club remains a vital tourism cog, enough to warrant city assistance when hotel developments forced Big Al's from its longtime home at 519 Main St. Other sites — on Hamilton Boulevard and the parking lot next to the Madison Theater — were met by opposition. But after lengthy debate and delays, the city created an alternative spot by selling Big Al's a parking lot at 400 SW Jefferson Ave. Opened in late 2012, the new building's 28,000 square feet dwarfs its 4,000-square-foot predecessor. The structure looks unassuming, almost utilitarian. But, as always, the neon sign outside easily and brightly identifies the business within.

CLUE FOR NEXT ITEM: You could trip over this peculiar barber pole.

The shop is gone, but barber pole lives on

Downtown Peoria's oddest sign says nothing.

And it's illegal. Not that it seems to be going anywhere.

A bulky, wooden barber pole juts from the sidewalk in front of 214 SW Jefferson Ave. — formerly Tooley's Barber Shop. In 1994, Jim Tooley relocated to the site, a sliver of a storefront, just 9 feet across, wedged between an old commercial building and a massive parking deck.

He hung out his shingle in two ways. He painted "TOOLEY'S" in big letters across the front of the shop. And he sunk the barber pole into the sidewalk. City Hall repeatedly told him it was illegal, but he and the pole stood their ground — until late 2013, that is. Tooley retired. But the pole stayed.

The shop is now a law office, for former Tooley customer Gary Morris. But the pole remains.

"It's kind of a unique feature there," Morris said just before moving in. "Maybe I'll paint it."

Nope. It's still blue, red and white.

CLUE FOR NEXT ITEM:
Big bird is no cartoon.

3 observation decks, a glass elevator — and one big ol' bird

At the Peoria Heights Observation Tower, the best view might be from the ground.

From that vantage, you can gaze at the village's most curious creature: a 300-pound, 6-foot-tall woodpecker. For five decades, it has been pecking a hole in the side of the 200-foot water tower, but thankfully hasn't made any headway — after all, a half-million gallons of water lurk inside.

The tower rises above — where else? — Tower Park, adjacent to Village Hall. The tower was built in 1968. A year later, in Vancouver Island, Canada, local philanthropist and conservationist Bill Rutherford spotted a massive woodpecker, carved by a chainsaw from a large, red cedar stump. He decided to bring it home, a souvenir for the entire Heights.

"My wife thought I was crazy for wanting to get the woodpecker," he once said. "But I thought it would be fun."

The big ol' bird was attached to the tower in 1970. Unlike its famous cartoon counterpart, this woodpecker remains nameless.

In addition to the oversized feathered friend, the tower hosts a glass elevator and three observation decks. Up top, telescopes allow a panoramic view of the Illinois River Valley; on a clear day, you can see 20 miles.

And on any day, you can see the woodpecker.

101 THINGS THAT PLAY IN PEORIA

CLUE FOR NEXT ITEM: Big appetite, small bun.

Ridiculous but delectable tenderloin is Peoria's 'Sandwich King'

It's one of the delightfully great mysteries of Peoria: Why the fascination with the pork tenderloin sandwich?

It's a deep-fried wonder, simple yet ubiquitous: tenderloin pounded thin, then breaded lightly and turned golden brown — and, apparently for overstated comedic effect, always served with one regulation-size hamburger bun.

It's said you can find them elsewhere in the Midwest, particularly Indiana — but not everywhere. For instance, sandwich-rife Chicago is not known for the tenderloin. But in Peoria, a great many restaurants boast their own.

No definitive history pinpoints the reason for the local, timeworn tenderloin affinity. To be sure, the late Hunt's drive-in long offered a beloved tenderloin. And the Village Inn in Spring Bay served a whopper of a tenderloin, until the eatery burned down in 2014.

These days, perhaps the most well known tenderloin lurks at Schooners, 730 E. War Memorial Drive in Peoria Heights. The joint has been cranking out foodstuffs for more than 30 years. In 2013, the Food Network's "Sandwich King" program stopped by to spotlight the tenderloin.

"It's 12 inches (in diameter) of meat, on a 4-inch bun," host Jeff Mauro said. "It's a perfect proportion."

101 THINGS THAT PLAY IN PEORIA

CLUE FOR NEXT ITEM:
Though yellow at heart, it can get really pushy.

Caterpillar bulldozers have global legacy of power, durability

If there's any machine that personifies the power, ruggedness and durability of Caterpillar Inc., it's the bulldozer.

Here's a machine that represents brute force.  Among the first machines manufactured here after Caterpillar Tractor Co. was formed in Peoria in 1925, bulldozers made history in World War II when the U.S. Army employed them to clear land for air strips and build roads in desolate areas.

Later, Caterpillar bulldozers were used to clear minefields and demolish enemy structures.

The bulldozer can be found today building roads, as well as being involved in logging, mining and farm work. The machine can climb steep banks to retrieve derailed rail cars and even locomotives, if necessary.

In 1956, several Caterpillar D8G bulldozers were commissioned to

take part in Operation Deep Freeze in Antarctica, pulling heavy cargo sleds and pushing snow. They were tough enough to stay on the job for almost 50 years before finally being retired from active duty.

Still manufactured in East Peoria, the D9, 10 and 11 models continue to be regarded as the Cadillacs of the bulldozer industry.

CLUE FOR NEXT ITEM: More than a century later, we still remember this ghost story.

Closing lid on this: There's peace at Old Book marker

Not long after the 1902 opening of the Illinois Asylum for the Incurable Insane, an unknown newcomer arrived.

He'd been working in a printing house when he suddenly could not speak. The illiterate man was dubbed A. Bookbinder or alternately, Manual Bookbinder — and affectionately known as Old Book.

At the Bartonville asylum, he was given a shovel and put on funeral detail. Each service, Book would lean on a tree and cry loudly.

In June 1910, Old Book died. At his funeral, as typical, the casket sat on crossbeams over an open grave. Two men on each side would grab the ends of two ropes under the casket and pull hard to slightly raise the heavy coffin. Another worker would slide out the crossbeams, and the straining crew would gently lower the coffin into the earth.

At Old Book's service, the men yanked the ropes. But there was no resistance by the coffin, and they stumbled and fell to the ground.

"The coffin ... bounded into the air, like an eggshell, as if it were empty," one account stated,

Onlookers heard a loud moaning: They saw Old Book leaning on a nearby tree, weeping. As workers pulled back the coffin's lid, Book's wailing ceased. Inside, Book lay peacefully.

101 THINGS THAT PLAY IN PEORIA

CLUE FOR NEXT ITEM: Floating time machine is a big deal with a big wheel.

Spirit of Peoria retains riverfront's link to city's past

Like a floating time machine, the Spirit of Peoria plies the Illinois River under paddlewheel power of yore.

The vessel is modeled after the steamboats of the mid-1880s, when Peoria's thriving riverfront would host multiple steamboats daily.

"The river is a huge part of Peoria," captain and owner Alex Grieves said in 2013, at the Spirit of Peoria's 25th anniversary celebration. "That's what put Peoria on the map, the Illinois River, and most towns would just love to be on the river."

The craft was built at the Walker Boat Yard in Paducah, Ky. The maiden crew needed four days to reach its destination, the dock at the foot of Peoria's Main Street.

The Spirit of Peoria arrived amid the fanfare of festive bands, media cameras and curious onlookers.

The boat is 160 feet long and four decks tall, with a passenger capacity of 487. Its dry weight is 275 tons, but it can carry 3,500 gallons of fuel and 2,500 gallons of water.

Propulsion comes solely via a paddlewheel, 21 feet in diameter. Average speed is 7 to 10 mph, depending on current, with a top speed of 15 mph.

Among its voyages, The Spirit of Peoria (spiritofpeoria.com) offers multi-day cruises far beyond central Illinois. But usually, the paddlewheeler can be spotted going up and down the river locally, maintaining a key vestige of local history.

101 THINGS THAT PLAY IN PEORIA

The Spirit of Peoria makes its way under the Murray Baker Bridge on the Illinois River. The vessel, modeled after steamboats of the mid-1880s, is propelled by a paddlewheel 21 feet in diameter and moves 7 to 10 mph on average, depending on current.

CLUE FOR NEXT ITEM: You say potato, I say po-tah-to, we all say delicious.

Neighbors gobbled up this homemade, salty treat

101 THINGS THAT PLAY IN PEORIA

With the Depression pushing in hard, Flossie Howard picked up a potato.

She peeled and sliced it by hand, then cooked the chips in a small, cast-iron kettle. She repeated the process until she got the recipe right in her Farmington home. When neighbors began gobbling and buying up her chips like mad, she and her family moved the burgeoning business to a former church in town.

Area communities clamored for the chips, and sales of Kitchen Cooked soared. For four decades, the family churned out chips. But when Flossie Howard's health failed, the company was sold to Richard Blackhurst of Hanna City.

In 1976, to expand production, a potato chip factory was built in Bushnell; two years later, another factory was built, in Farmington. The company's 90 employees make multiple varieties of snacks, including pretzels, cheese curls and tortilla chips (available online: kitchencooked.net).

In 2003, Esquire magazine, in an article titled "The Best Potato Chips You Never Tasted," ranked Kitchen Cooked chips second in a national taste test of regional chip makers. The writer described the chips as "almost too beautiful to eat."

CLUE FOR NEXT ITEM: You could get hooked by this sculpture.

Sonar Tide makes artistic statement at Civic Center

In 1981, art got laughed away from the Peoria Civic Center.

A proposed outdoor sculpture, by New York City artist Richard Serra, involved 40-foot dual steel towers shaped in an offset V — and destined to rust. A public outcry against the idea — detractors dubbed it "The Shaft" — prompted the Civic Center Authority to reject the proposal.

That paved the way for Sonar Tide, designed by another New York sculptor, Ronald Bladen, considered a "father of minimalism." Later, in describing his conception of the work, he recalled, "I immediately saw a curve when I came to Peoria. I wanted to retain the openness and freedom and not split the plaza."

101 THINGS THAT PLAY IN PEORIA

Sonar Tide received favorable public reaction. Critics lauded it as Bladen's finest design to date.

The massive work, fabricated by local craftsman Daniel Van Buskirk, was dedicated May 23, 1983. Consisting of 14 tons of welded steel, it stretches more than 51 feet long and 26 feet high.

The project was made possible by $50,000 raised by the Junior League of Peoria. The sum was matched by the National Endowment of the Arts.

Bladen died in 1988. Van Buskirk died in 1992.

CLUE FOR NEXT ITEM: Peoria, the center of the universe? See the proof.

Peoria's model of the universe stretches from here to WIU

![101 THINGS THAT PLAY IN PEORIA]

Locals like to joke that Peoria is the hub of the universe, but it's surely true at the Peoria Riverfront Museum.

There, you'll find a 46-foot-diameter sun — the center of the Community Solar System. It's recognized by the Guinness Book of Records as the world's largest scale model of our neck of the universe.

The scale factor is 99,000,000:1, spread across 6,000 square miles of central Illinois. The closet planet is Mercury, 4.8 inches in diameter and located near the playground at the RiverPlex, 0.36 miles away from the museum. Earth

CLUE FOR NEXT ITEM:
It's a shoe-in as the shiniest place in Peoria.

is 5 inches and 0.94 miles away, at Constitution Park.

The biggest planet, Jupiter, is 55 inches in diameter and 4.9 miles away, hanging in the lobby at Gen. Wayne A. Downing Peoria International Airport. Other planets are in Pekin, Princeville and Wyoming.

Of several dwarf planets, Pluto is 0.9 inches in diameter and located 40 miles away at Good's Furniture in Kewanee. The farthest outpost is another dwarf planet, Eris, which is 0.9 inches in diameter and located 62 miles away at Western Illinois University's Horrabin Hall.

A complete rundown of the model can be found at www.peoriariverfrontmuseum.org/dome-planetarium/community-solar-system.

Get a snappy shine from George Manias Downtown

In Peoria, there's no snap as sweet as a rag cracked at the end of a shoe shine by George Manias.

It marks the sharp finale of another masterwork by the shine maestro, Manias — the CEO (and everything else) at George's Shoeshine & Hatters.

In 1946, 15-year-old Manias grabbed a rag and started shining shoes — 20 cents per customer — inside a Downtown barbershop. Then as now, he dressed sharp, with a bow tie, to set him apart from the competition.

"I put everybody out of business," he once said.

By 1951, he'd saved enough money to open a nine-chair parlor inside the Niagara Hotel. He has been at 101 SW Adams St. since 1989.

Manias has hosted a legion of political luminaries, including presidents Barack Obama, George W. Bush, Ronald Reagan and Gerald Ford.

He may be the hardest working man in shoe business. In 2013, he had a heart attack, yet returned just 11 days later. By best estimate, he has shined more than 1 million shoes — and counting.

At the sound of that final crack, Manias will pause to glance over his handiwork. He'd ask, "How's that?"

Perfect, George. As always.

101 THINGS THAT PLAY IN PEORIA

CLUE FOR NEXT ITEM:
He once cast a pall of fear across Peoria,
but now just gazes across a bar.

Bernie Shelton still has his place at his tavern

At one time, Bernie Shelton cast a pall of fear across Peoria.

Now, he just gazes across a bar — unless you believe in ghosts.

As in days of yore, you can find him at 2016 W. Farmington Road in West Peoria. Atop a wall inside Kenny's Westside Pub, a drawing of Shelton stands as a simple reminder of his infamy here.

During the '40s heyday of the Shelton Gang, Bernie Shelton owned the squat bar, then known as the Parkway Tavern. He was the muscle of the gambling-centric gang, run by brother Carl Shelton.

But by 1947, Carl Shelton had quit the rackets, retiring to the family farm in southern Illinois. There, he was gunned down Oct. 23, 1947.

Bernie Shelton still held court at his tavern. On the morning of July 26, 1948, he stepped outside and heard a lone rifle crack from the bluff behind the tap. Shelton died not long afterward.

The Parkway continued on, changing names in modern times and becoming Kenny's in 2013. Despite an interior rehab, the staff reports a holdover manifestation: lights flicker, things move — allegedly the handiwork of Bernie Shelton's unsettled ghost.

101 THINGS THAT PLAY IN PEORIA

CLUE FOR NEXT ITEM: You'll be green with envy if you don't join these revelers.

Peoria's St. Patrick's Day parade is the city's largest street party

Peoria's biggest street party occurs during the annual St. Patrick's Day Parade.

Actually, revelers aren't supposed to be in the street. Most imbibers abide, staying on the sidewalks and out of the way of the parade, which in recent years has exploded in popularity.

In its younger years, the parade (which the St. Patrick's Society debuted in 1989) had enough floats to last maybe a half-hour. Nowadays, the procession includes more than 100 floats and marches through Downtown for more than an hour — before crowds of thousands and thousands of onlookers lining various streets, crammed tight on many sidewalks.

The biggest throng reverberates along the 500 block of Main Street, home to several bars. There, in 2011, police took to painting lines on the street to keep spectators out of the way of floats. To that end, police on bicycles and horseback also try to convince partygoers to stay out of harm's way.

For the most part, the beer-happy crowd is enthusiastic but behaved: It's not as if the National Guard is on stand-by. And though the likes of Boston and Savannah can boast bigger and crazier St. Pat's shenanigans, on at least one day a year — sure and begorrah — Peoria bursts out with a street party worthy of any big city.

101 THINGS THAT PLAY IN PEORIA

CLUE FOR NEXT ITEM: Beer-drinking of another heritage will earn you notoriety in this pub.

Hofbrau still providing time, room for beer club

Whereas some people see beer as a beverage, others see it as a pastime.

And for some, it's even more than that, almost a sport.

Witness the Peoria Hofbrau, 2210 NE Jefferson Ave. Since 1984, the pub has been serving authentic German fare, plus a wide selection of imported and craft beers. Long before the micro-brew explosion, the Hofbrau stood as a reliable outpost for hard-to-find beers.

In the '80s, the Hofbrau created its beer club. Participation was simple: Drink a beer, get a card stamped — but only one brand per card. Drink 50 different beers — no time limit — and you get your name on a small plaque on the wall.

Over time, the threshold has risen repeatedly. Otherwise, the Hofbrau could run out of wall space. Currently, you need to hit 100 beers to get your name on the wall.

Some names appear once. Many appear multiple times. One is up there 100 times. Yes, 100.

Most Hofbrau beers run $4.50 to $6.95. Multiply that by 100. That's a sizable investment — yet one many beer aficionados gladly pay. For them, with the fervor of an Olympic athlete chasing the gold, it's all about the Hofbrau plaque.

CLUE FOR NEXT ITEM: Fans would buy this sandwich if it were made only of bread.

Avanti's Gondola is River City's signature sandwich

No food item claims a more singular identity with Peoria than the Avanti's Gondola.

Countless Peorians who've moved away, to points all over the world, make Avanti's their first stop when visiting their hometown. Avanti's owner Albert Zeller hears their stories all the time.

"People say, 'We came here straight from the airport, because we have to have Gondolas,'" Zeller says.

The Gondola looks like any other elongated submarine sandwich based with ham, salami, cheese and lettuce. But the first bite betrays the eyes.

"Of course," Zeller says,

101 THINGS THAT PLAY IN PEORIA

"it's the bread. Bread-making is quite a science."

The 16-inch Gondola already was on the menu in 1966, when Zeller bought Lavadona's, on the southwest corner of Main and University streets, and renamed it Avanti's. Zeller kept the sandwich but changed the bread, which is made fresh daily.

Now the Gondola is the signature dish for Avanti's, which includes six stores. At one time, Zeller says, the full-service restaurant off Sterling and Glen avenues was selling 18,000 Gondolas monthly.

And "Gondola" is trademarked, along with Avanti's motto: "Home of the Famous Gondola."

CLUE FOR NEXT ITEM:
Seats to the best view around.

Bully! Grandview Drive's the place to sit and soak it in

Perhaps Teddy Roosevelt didn't do Grandview Drive right.

To be sure, he gave the winding road its signature tag. When in town for a 1910 speech, as his touring car bounded high above the Illinois River valley, his driver apologized for adverse road conditions. The former president famously replied, "What difference does it make? I have traveled all over the world, and this is the world's most beautiful drive."

Nice tip of the cap. But just think of how Roosevelt might've felt had he taken the time to step out of his car, sit a spell and take in the view.

That's the magic of the Grandview Drive benches, each a simple spot to stop and stare.

The 2.5-mile road, built in 1903 and part of the Peoria Park District, is the only linear park on the National Historic Register. The valley side of the road is owned by the park district, which is undeveloped except for occasional benches.

Most days, you can see the pavement shared by bouncing joggers, leashed dogs,

eager shutterbugs and impatient cars. But the true view connoisseurs, including folks seeking a brief slice of solace in the middle of a busy workday, know that there's no better way to appreciate Grandview than from one of those plain, peaceful benches.

CLUE FOR NEXT ITEM:
For this guess, the writing is on the wall.

40

Mural features local personalities enjoying Mardi Gras

At State and Water streets, you'll find a perpetual "Animal House" party scene.

But no worries: the shindig never gets off-the-wall. That's because it's *on* the wall.

A mural — 50 feet long by 17 feet high — graces a corner of the five-building complex that goes by the name Le Vieux Carre (French for "The Old Square"). The 2000 work, by artists Lonnie Stewart and Mariam Graff, sports a Mardi Gras theme as a nod to the French history of the riverfront. The work traces traditions of Mardi Gras, with stops in Greece, France, Italy and New Orleans. Leopards, pigs and peacocks mingle with raucous, dancing revelers.

The mural also includes several local personalities. The most obvious is late councilman Gary Sandberg — a stand-in for Bacchus, the Roman god of wine — astride a mule. He wears a crown of grapes and carries a goblet in one hand and a daisy in the other. One eyebrow cocked slyly, he seems to know that this party will never end.

101 THINGS THAT PLAY IN PEORIA

CLUE FOR NEXT ITEM: Why does this beast look so mean? Maybe he needs a cup of coffee.

Black bear fits right in at current Peoria home

Generations of Peorians will recall the Jumer's bear. But for younger Peorians, it's the thirty-thirty bear.

The name doesn't matter. We're just glad it's out of hibernation.

The stuffed black bear long stood near the lobby of Jumer's Castle Lodge, 117 N. Western Ave. The motionless but ferocious critter was the namesake of the Black Bear Lounge, home to the piano stylings of Jimmy Binkley.

After changing hands, the inn folded in 2009. By then, the Jumer family had exited the business, taking the black bear along and putting it in storage.

Two years later, the thirty-thirty Coffee Co. opened at the Kickapoo Building at 734 Main St., owned by the Jumer family. As thirty-thirty prepared to move in, the owners threw an idea at their landlords.

"We asked what the bear was doing," says Ty Paluska. "It's such an iconic Peoria figure. But it was in storage.

"We looked at it for two reasons: for branding the business, and to bring back a part of Peoria history."

The Jumers blessed the idea, and the black bear took a spot just inside an entrance. Mouth agape and arms wide, the bear is photographed likely more than any other two-legged creature in Peoria.

101 THINGS THAT PLAY IN PEORIA

CLUE FOR NEXT ITEM: We share the tail of these furry campus favorites.

Bold squirrels an approachable — and hungry — fixture at Bradley

On the quad at Bradley University, students appreciate the friendly, ubiquitous squirrels.

It's not exactly like roses: One does not stop and smell the squirrels. Then again, some Bradley squirrels — tamer and/or braver than most — probably wouldn't mind a sniff, especially in exchange for a bite to eat.

Other campuses have squirrels. But Bradley's are particularly nimble and approachable. When hungry, they scamper right up to you, patiently pausing in silent begging.

Some students feed the creatures regularly. One story holds that a student in a second-floor dorm liked to feed the rodents but didn't like to schlep outside. So he rigged a pulley system from his window. Every morning at 8 a.m., he'd turn a hand-crank and send down a cup of nuts. At precisely that time a squirrel — the same squirrel every day — would show up for breakfast.

In 2004, a now-defunct website called Campus Squirrel Listings ranked schools on the basis of the squirrel population. BU got a four-squirrel-head ranking, the highest possible: "Home to the fox squirrel, the Bradley campus is host to a number of people-approaching, nut-begging, and sometimes snack-insistent squirrel personalities. ... Squirrel presence throughout the park-like campus is robust."

Is there any wonder some BU fans have pushed for the squirrel as a school mascot?

101 THINGS THAT PLAY IN PEORIA

CLUE FOR NEXT ITEM:
On hot summer days, you might want to take a shower — outside.

One of city's coolest spots started off as dry idea

Was there actually a time when you couldn't beat the heat in the Gateway Building fountain?

The sprinkler has become a Peoria summer staple, offering sweet relief when temperatures skyrocket. The fountain mostly serves as a kiddie

playground. But if the sun is blistering, don't be surprised to see parents and other adults meandering through the cooling water.

Yet the original plans were dry for the city's $7 million renovation project at 200 NE Water St., at the foot of Hamilton Boulevard. The Gateway Building was envisioned as a public conference center with no fountain.

However, before the 1996 groundbreaking, the Illinois Riverfront Development Corp. received a $125,000 donation from Gordon and Jean Peters to build a fountain in the plaza in honor of their parents.

"Our parents believed and taught us that everyone should be prepared

in any way they can to give something back to their community," Gordon Peters said at the time.

The fountain, along with the rest of the project, opened in 1997. Ever since, it has been one of the coolest spots in Peoria.

CLUE FOR NEXT ITEM: It's perhaps the biggest and highest local symbol of a holiday nine months away.

Festival of Lights wreath stands as star atop East Peoria

Of the countless bulbs and changing displays for the East Peoria Festival of Lights, none has shined as brightly as the wreath atop Fondulac Drive.

For 30 years, the wreath — like the star atop a Christmas tree — has served as the highest hallmark of the holiday event.

Fest aficionados know many of the iconic displays, such as the Starship Enterprise and

ski jumper. And certainly the FOLEPI soldier stands strong as the mascot.

But, for passers-by on Interstate 74 and Illinois Route 116, along with other nearby routes, the wreath heralds the start of the holiday season. It's become a local tradition: When the wreath is first flipped on, fest fans know the Winter Wonderland is open for drive-through.

For years, the wreath had been fashioned from a small Ferris wheel that the city of East Peoria would borrow and decorate each year. But in 2014, the city crafted a new wreath, complete with LED lights and a timer. The wreath — $20,000 for the structure and $10,000 for the lights — glimmers brighter than ever before.

CLUE FOR NEXT ITEM: Ducks paddle in Pekin, but people keep their feet dry inside this mode of transportation.

Pekin's Mineral Springs Park a busy place, with paddleboats at its heart

Mineral Springs Park and Lagoon can mean a lot of things to different visitors.

Offerings include a skate park, dog park, bike trail, playground, tennis courts, picnic grills and bocce ball. Plus, you can find anglers (often kids) dunking a fishing line into the stocked lagoon.

And the park — especially around the lagoon — is loaded with ducks. They lounge around the water and, occasionally, a pair will waddle along the sidewalk, hogging the concrete as if they own it. Few people seem to mind, though. Most walkers and runners will smile and veer off to the side, leaving the ducks to roam free.

Often, parents and kids will stop on the way to the park to buy discount bread to feed the ducks, which never seem to wither of appetite. That's a

likely reason they never leave.

But the trademark of Mineral Springs would be the paddleboats. You know it's summertime (or thereabouts) when visitors rent a boat to pedal through the lagoon. The ducks don't seem to mind the company.

CLUE FOR NEXT ITEM:
This football-shaped sign shows that sports play big in Peoria.

Peoria Stadium pigskin a sign of prep football pride

The big, brown football salutes countless cars daily along War Memorial Drive.

The sign, plus the fields behind it, triggers modern memories of gridiron rivalries, track meets and softball games. But the history of Peoria Stadium includes much more.

In 1895, the site was developed from farmland into a horse track. Over time, buildings sprang up for more uses, such as hog shows, airplane exhibitions, auto races and religious revivals. A final fling with wagering involved greyhounds, starting in 1926. But the Depression shut down the track in 1931.

Yet new life came five years later. The Peoria School Board spent $300,000 to buy the land and create a football field and quarter-mile track. The grounds became a mecca for local sports. The American Legion hosted a yearly July 4 fireworks display.

By the 1970s, the site — dubbed Peoria Public Schools Stadium — had fallen into disrepair. The grandstand was destined for condemnation, but community fundraisers came up with just enough money to cover bare-bones repairs.

In recent years, the district has considered selling the land, possibly to Wal-Mart Stores Inc., for development. But bolstered by public outcry against such a move, Peoria Stadium has survived.

CLUE FOR NEXT ITEM:
What'll you have? A big blue logo.

Tribute to the days when the brewery was king

For more than a half-century, the Pabst Blue Ribbon brewery stood as the dominant industry in Peoria Heights.

Generations of residents learned to live with the smell of malt, along with traffic halts when the brewery's semi-trailers backed onto Prospect Road. For many, a job at Pabst seemed as secure a job as any. Thus, the 1982 shutdown resounded like a death knell.

But the Heights rebounded, with a main drag now replete with upscale shops and eateries. Part of the gentrification is the Pabst Building, 4541 N. Prospect Ave. Up top, you can still see the bright PBR logo.

Most of the brewery operation was demolished over time, but the brick bastion survives (and thrives) as a four-story professional building with varied tenants. Pettet Jewelry inhabits the old "33 Room," the hospitality hall named after Pabst's claim that it took "33 separate brews to put such flavor, such smoothness, such unvarying goodness into a single glass of Blue Ribbon."

More than three decades after the brewery's closure, the mention of Pabst still engenders resentment from some quarters. Still, there's no denying the beer's long and strong role in the village's history. And the blue logo still stands tall, overlooking the town.

101 THINGS THAT PLAY IN PEORIA

CLUE FOR NEXT ITEM: Not one but many things define the chockablock interior decor of this Irish mainstay.

Jimmy's Bar was kitschy when kitschy wasn't cool

There's no "thing" at Jimmy's Bar. Rather, it's things, with an "s."

In recent times, it's become common at chain eateries to cram walls with chockablock decor — antiques, kitsch, whatever — to exude a convivial, carefree atmosphere. But Jimmy's Bar, rarely known to set national trends, has been ahead of the hodgepodge-decor curve since its doors opened in 1982.

In fact, the walls of the bar, 2801 W. Farmington Road in West Peoria, became so jammed that Jimmy Spears had to post mementoes on the ceiling — and now that's full, too. There's no rhyme or reason to the chaotic smear, though most are Irish or sporting.

To wit: Guinness sign. "Erin Go Bragh" poster. Mike Ditka 8-by-10. Rivermen jersey. Neon shamrock. Large Irish flag. Guinness pennant. Small Irish flag. Hurling stick. Marcus Pollard football jersey. Guinness flag. Chicago Blackhawks 2013 Stanley Cup tapestry. Jimmy Buffett handbill for show at Robertson Memorial Field House. Guinness mirror. Sign pointing 5 kilometers to Clonmel, Peoria's Irish sister city. Various high school pennants. Guinness magazine ad suggesting, "Try a Guinness."

And, just in case you somehow forget where you are, multiple signs proclaim "Jimmy's Bar."

101 THINGS THAT PLAY IN PEORIA

CLUE FOR NEXT ITEM:
This sign is well red along Peoria's skyline.

Red block letters shine through good times, bad

Perhaps no sign is more iconic to the Peoria skyline than the red, bold "HOTEL PERE MARQUETTE."

The block letters beckon to the east and west. Their look and longevity testify to two Peoria traits: unpretentious and dependable.

101 THINGS THAT PLAY IN PEORIA

The hotel opened on Jan. 5, 1927. About 16,000 visitors gawked at 501 Main St., where 14 stories and 375 rooms had been built for a princely $2.5 million. A night's lodging was $2.50, while a 16-ounce T-bone steak cost $2.25.

The name of the Hotel Pere Marquette was selected from 41,000 contest entries. The winner — Mrs. H.M. Kipp of 218 North St. — suggested Father Jacques Marquette, the French explorer who journeyed down the Illinois River in 1673.

Over the years, the swank hotel hosted big names, including Helen Hayes, Eddie Cantor, Lady Bird Johnson, Lawrence Welk, Bob Hope, Dwight Eisenhower and John F. Kennedy. In the late 1970s, the

Pere hit hard times as a Hilton affiliate, closing its doors in 1980. But it reopened a year later and enjoyed a resurgence under new ownership.

The site went dark again in December 2011, as part of a $100 hotel project Downtown. The hotel reopened in June 2013 as the Marriott Pere Marquette.

The red letters are back on again.

CLUE FOR NEXT ITEM:
This sweet treat has been gobbled in Peoria for generations.

50

Trefzger's has left its thumbprint on Peoria history

Trefzger's Bakery presented one of the biggest challenges regarding the rigorous selection process for "101 Things."

Which signature item to pick: the thumbprint cookies or coffee cakes? We eventually opted for the cookies, if only for the frosting. We like that frosting best.

But either treat represents a sweet history that goes back to 1861, the year the bakery was founded Downtown by Simon Trefzger. The German immi-

grant had been awarded a contract to make loaves of bread for Union troops training near what today is Glen Oak Park. As he expanded his offerings, cakes and other sweets eventually joined the menu.

In 1953, the baker moved to 3504 N. Prospect Road. Forty years later, the fourth generation of Trefzgers retired and sold the business to pastry chef Jeff Huebner. He and wife Martha continue with most of the Trefzger traditions.

"We introduced a few new things but tried to keep everything the way it was," Huebner once said. "It had been working so well already. Why mess with a good thing?"

That good thing is on the move again, to a new location in Peoria Heights. Still, it'll be the same Trefzger's, same recipes and same thumbprint cookies.

CLUE FOR NEXT ITEM:
This bike has traveled, but still hails Heights history.

Bicycle clock marks history in manufacturing

When Kelly Avenue School closed in 2001, an era ended in Peoria Heights.

For about 165 years, a school had been located along Prospect Road. Back then, it was called Mount Hawley Road, in the middle of which was plunked a log schoolhouse. Two other schools opened before a one-room, wood-frame school opened at the Kelly Avenue site in 1896, two years before Peoria Heights was incorporated.

In 1916, the anchor of the current brick school was built at the same location. The Kelly Street School had eight classrooms and a basement. The east wing was added in 1924 and the west wing three years later.

101 THINGS THAT PLAY IN PEORIA

Along the way, the school adopted an icon: a bicycle clock, a nod to the village's history in bike manufacturing. The big bicycle faced Prospect Road, viewed by countless cars every day.

In the 1990s, plans arose for a new school campus on Glen Avenue, with separate buildings for a high school and grade school. The latter would combine Kelly Avenue and Monroe schools.

Kelly Avenue School and its 3½ acres were sold to make way for retail space. But the clock survived.

It now adorns Peoria Heights Grade School, 500 E. Glen Ave. Just like the old days, endless passers-by glimpse at the bicycle clock every day.

CLUE FOR NEXT ITEM: Peoria is no desert, but motorists can spy one prickly plant.

Green cactus guides people to concrete supply store

You don't see many cacti in Peoria. Maybe in Peoria, Ariz. But not Peoria, Ill.

But there's a cactus in front of 3020 SW Adams St., the handiwork of S&G Decorative Concrete Supply.

The brick structure first functioned as a barn for street cars, starting in 1903. A hundred years later, S&G moved in. The next year, the cactus was born, says Christi Shaw, who owns the place with her husband, Ron.

"It was a Friday night, the guys were bored and they had a lot of extra concrete," she says with a laugh.

Her husband suggested a cactus "just because," she says. Using vertical concrete, which can be sculpted, the crew fashioned a cactus in the parkway along Adams Street. Later, it was painted green and dotted with small scorpions.

"If you're out in the desert, there are probably going to be some scorpions," Shaw says.

Passers-by stop to take photos with the cactus. Some top it with hats. Many paint faces.

"We're always repainting it," she says.

But it's worth the work, as the cactus serves as a valuable signpost. When customers call for directions, Shaw tells them to look for the green cactus.

101 THINGS THAT PLAY IN PEORIA

A cactus made of concrete on Adams Street welcomes visitors to S&G Decorative Concrete Supply.

The usual reply: "We know where that is! We've always wondered what the story was with that."

CLUE FOR NEXT ITEM: For this garden, a dairy farmer piled up rocks for 20 years — then piled up more.

Jubilee Rock Garden: From quirky dream to labor of love

William Notzke had rocks in his head — as well as his truck, hands and yard.

It was all part of a unique dream. In the 1930s, west of Kickapoo on U.S. Route 150, he ran the Jubilee Dairy, which touted the "best ice cream in Peoria County." Meanwhile, he got a vision to create an on-site rock garden.

So, in 1939, he began taking trips in his pickup to Colorado and Arkansas,

hauling back ton after ton of quartz. Over two decades, Notzke built a five-level, pink-and-white rock garden — walls, ropes, sculptings — out of rose and crystal quartz.

His wife, Ethel, didn't much care for his handiwork. Still, after she died in 1964, he started working on the site's crowning element: a memorial arch in her name. The arch was electronically wired to allow lights to shine through diamond- and heart-shaped openings. A copper plate reads, "This monument designed and built by W.A. Notzke in memory of my beloved wife Ethel M. Notzke. 1894-1963."

After he died at age 89 in 1991, his

daughter sold the place to Cheryl and John Becker, who have been caretakers ever since. Though parts deteriorated beyond repair, they've maintained the spread as created.

Visitors are invited to stop by. But be kind: It's private property.

CLUE FOR NEXT ITEM:
By the dozen, these round and tasty treats are an autumn tradition.

Tanner's apple cider doughnuts are in demand

Tanner's Orchard has come to symbolize fall for many across central Illinois.

The 80-acre farm is located in Speer, about 20 miles north of Peoria on Illinois Route 40. Apples are king. You can buy a basket of them or climb one of the 11,000 trees on the grounds and gather your own.

Free apple cider greets you when you enter the Tanner's building, but then something else hits you: the scent of apple cider doughnuts baked on the premises. Regardless of what you may have heard about fats and nutrition, consumption of these doughnuts is mandatory.

Two years ago, Tanner's had to install another doughnut machine to keep up with weekend demand, said Jennifer Beaver, a manager at the orchard.

As urban America moves further from our agrarian roots — even in the middle of the Corn Belt — Tanner's has come to provide that weekend return to the farm and all the romantic notions that go with it. They've also helped restore one's faith in doughnuts. Last year, Tanner's sold 44,000 dozen of these apple cider rings. That's more than half-a-million doughnuts — and the place is only open a few months out of the year. Beyond local sales, shipments go not just across the country but all over the world.

Owned and operated by

the Tanner family since 1947, Tanner's Orchard is home to all kinds of apples, farm animals, a corn maze and lots of jams and jellies. But it's the apple cider doughnuts that draw people like a moth to the proverbial flame.

A 40-mile round trip for a doughnut? Make that a dozen. Opening day for doughnuts is July 20, by the way.

CLUE FOR NEXT ITEM:
This sign of salvation is especially bright on Easter.

Shining sign of rescue, refuge since 1962

With "Jesus Saves," a simple sign offers a throwback look and future hope.

In 1955, two Peoria women, Florence Holzschuh and Helen Durdel, witnessed a Chicago mission in action. Back home, they and their businessmen husbands bought Grim's Clothing Store at 510 SW Adams St. There, they opened Peoria City Mission and began serving coffee and rolls to the hungry and homeless men of Peoria.

Over the next few years, the need for more space prompted a move to 601 SW Adams St., big enough for food storage, showers and beds. There, the name was changed to Peoria Rescue Ministries.

In 1962, Holzschuh died. Her memorial funds purchased the neon cross beckoning, "Jesus Saves."

Since then, Peoria Rescue Ministries has increased its services, to women as well as men. The sign remains a constant, still bright as ever.

CLUE FOR NEXT ITEM: Looking for heavy fire power? You'll find a sidewalk arsenal Downtown.

Distillery baron took best shot, has been rewarded since

In sabre-rattling fashion, it's somehow comforting to see 20 cannonballs stockpiled in Downtown Peoria.

They're stationed next to a cannon outside the Grand Army of the Republic Hall, 416 Hamilton Blvd. The weaponry is at little risk for theft: The cannonballs each weigh 110 pounds, while the muzzle-loading cannon, which was used in Atlantic Coast defense during the Civil War, weighs 7,000 pounds.

The hall was originally named after Joseph B. Greenhut, a Peoria distillery baron. Greenhut, who had organized his own Civil War infantry company, contributed $14,000 to build a hall that cost $22,000. ("Greenhut Memorial" is still carved in stone above the entrance.) At a dedication on Dec. 30, 1909, Greenhut told fellow Union vets, "If you have as much pleasure in your meetings and sociables as I have had in helping, I am well repaid."

The hall served for years as a meeting place for members of the Grand Army of the Republic, along with associated groups. But after they died out, so did their sons and daughters. In 1972, with the site deteriorating, the new Central Illinois Landmarks Foundation raised money and took over the hall.

Today, the hall is rented out for banquets and other events — cannonballs included.

101 THINGS THAT PLAY IN PEORIA

CLUE FOR NEXT ITEM:
Speaking of the military, this memorial was put back together like Humpty Dumpty.

57

Memorial pays tribute to soldiers and Averyville

Averyville was a proud village.

In 1919, its 3,800-some residents created the Patriotic Relief Association to help families suffering because of casualties of World War I (then, of course, called simply the World War). The group solicited contributions, some of which went toward building a memorial, dubbed simply the World War Soldiers and Sailors of Averyville Monument. The 25-foot-tall the memorial, which included four bronze tablets bearing the names of veterans of the war, rose from the base of Grandview Drive.

In 1926, Averyville was annexed by Peoria. Eventually, the monument area became part of the Peoria Park District.

Over time, weather wore down the marker, with lightning zapping the eagle up top. So, in 2013, the park district decided to repair the marker. But it consisted mostly of terra cotta, a clay-like material with which no American restorer had much experience. So, piece by piece — 175 in all — the memorial was taken apart and sent — by truck, then ship — to an expert terra-cotta firm in England. Total cost: $214,000.

Last year, the park district put the puzzle back together. The memorial is back in its original spot, with the original tablets — which pay tribute not just to the fallen soldiers but to a village that is gone, as well.

101 THINGS THAT PLAY IN PEORIA

CLUE FOR NEXT ITEM:
Four scary faces protect one key resource.

Warding off 'evil spirits' to keep city water clean

Next time you drink tap water in Peoria, thank a "gargoyle."

That's according to the legend at Illinois-American Water Co., where a quartet of grotesques protects the place by defiantly sticking out their tongues.

The fearsome foursome are poised atop the Main Pumping Station, located on Lorentz Street, north of the McClugage Bridge. Built in 1890, the station is a handsome example of the Romanesque Revival architectural style featuring red sandstone with elaborate carvings, stained glass windows, copper flashing, hardwood trim

101 THINGS THAT PLAY IN PEORIA

and turrets.

The front of the building is etched "Peoria Water Works Company," from which descended Illinois-American Water Co. The Main Pumping Station, which now houses a company museum, is on the National Register of Historic Places.

Meanwhile, the four "gargoyles" continue to stand sentinel at each corner of the flat roof. Made of zinc, they ward off "evil spirits," according to a plaque on the building. For more than a century up there, they — along with their menacing tongues — have done a good job.

CLUE FOR NEXT ITEM:
He's forever ready for Opening Day in Peoria.

Pete Vonachen still greeting young fans at Dozer Park

Though Peoria lost its godfather of minor league baseball in 2013, Pete Vonachen's gregarious presence remains larger than life at Dozer Park.

In 2005, to celebrate Vonachen's 80th birthday, a one-ton statue was unveiled on the ballpark's concourse. The work, by renowned Peoria artist Lonnie Stewart, shows Vonachen in a common goodwill gesture: presenting a baseball to a youngster.

"You all thought you were going to get rid of me, but now you can't," Vonachen joked at the presentation ceremony.

Then he turned serious, adding, "This is the greatest moment of my life. In the words of the late Lou Gehrig, I consider myself the luckiest guy on the face of the earth at this moment."

The occasion also prompted Vonachen to reference his late best friend, Harry Caray, at whose 1998 funeral Vonachen delivered a memorable funny/tender eulogy. After seeing the new statue, Vonachen pointed to the sky and blurted, "OK, wise guy, you got a statue (at Wrigley Field). Now I got one, too!"

The Vonachen statue stands not far from the ballpark entrance, greeting endless streams of baseball fans, just like old times.

101 THINGS THAT PLAY IN PEORIA

Flowers and baseballs with messages of condolences are seen at the statue of Harold "Pete" Vonachen at the entrance of Dozer Park on June 10, 2013 — the day he died at the age of 87.

CLUE FOR NEXT ITEM: Now lying down, Peoria's biggest tree wasn't born here.

Tree in Detweiller is a piece of California in Peoria

Did Paul Bunyan and his ax visit Detweiller Park?

It's a reasonable question as you motor along the park's main entrance and encounter a felled tree far more massive than anything you'd spot in the outlying woods.

That's because the tree isn't local. It's a chunk of redwood hauled from California a century ago.

In 1915, The Holt Caterpillar Co. wanted to demonstrate the power of its crawler-type equipment. For that purpose, the redwood was brought to the company's East Peoria plant.

After the tree was nudged around, it was left to stand decoratively as a two-part display in front of the plant. Later, it was donated to the Peoria Park District and relocated to Detweiller Park.

The park itself was a gift by Thomas Detweiller, who purchased the 661-acre Payson Farm and renamed it in honor of his father, pioneer steamboat Capt. Henry Detweiller. The park was dedicated in 1928.

Over time, the redwood began to lose its bark. For a while, the park district nailed pieces of bark back onto the tree. Eventually, the park district abandoned the losing effort and let the tree become naturally nude.

101 THINGS THAT PLAY IN PEORIA

A felled redwood tree is displayed at Detweiller Park. The tree, which was brought over from California in 1915, was once displayed in front of the Caterpillar plant in East Peoria before being relocated to Detweiller Park.

CLUE FOR NEXT ITEM: Speaking of parks, these blufftop vantage spots are not parking lots.

Fondulac Drive lookouts are mini parks with mighty views

Where some might see parking lots, others see parks.

That's what you'll find along Fondulac Drive in East Peoria. The scenic drive includes two simple spots of gravel — known as lookouts — that are owned and maintained by the Fondulac Park District.

101 THINGS THAT PLAY IN PEORIA

The lookouts have sat alongside the winding road since the 1930s. One is essentially a wide shoulder running about one-eighth of a mile in the 900 block. The other, a square plot capable of accommodating several cars, stretches next to the bridge over Interstate 74; that's the site of the Festival of Lights wreath each yuletide.

During special occasions, such as Independence Day, the lookouts become crammed with cars as people jockey for position to watch fireworks. Most days, though, just a smattering of motorists will stop by to take a breather, read a book or enjoy the view.

CLUE FOR NEXT ITEM: Vroom! Kids know this circle of fun is the only one of its kind in the Peoria area.

Kartville still on go after more than half century

For more than a half-century, one of the sweetest sounds of summer buzzes out of the hollow off the Swords Avenue Hill.

As you get close, you'll hear a whine, like a nest of bees in the distance, gradually increasing as a mass murmur, then ZZZZZOOOOM-ING by, fading in the wake of a dust cloud.

Welcome to Kartville, a throwback slice of Americana and the only place in the area to find a go-kart.

The 23-acre park — which also offers batting cages, dune buggies, mini-golf and bumper boats — has been pretty much the same since 1963. That's when Al Baker cleaned up a weed-choked, abandoned go-kart track at 919 N. Swords Ave. At the time, there were five go-kart tracks in Peoria, but all others have died off, victims of increased insurance rates and other entertainment options.

The place is now owned by the originator's son, David Baker, who grew up at the track. Like the Kartville faithful, he passed on his go-kart affinity to his kids, then to a third generation.

In that way, Kartville survives as a rare multigenerational bond. It's hard for grandparents and grandchildren to find an entertainment touchstone. But March through November, you can find kids of all ages smiling behind the wheel of a Kartville go-kart.

CLUE FOR NEXT ITEM:
Now near a famous Peoria tree, this fountain once helped horses and humans.

Easton left legacy of watering oases in city

At the turn of the 20th Century, travelers periodically had to pull over and fill up.

Not with gasoline. With water.

Yet when horses were still a main mode of transportation, riders sometimes had a hard time finding Peoria watering oases. Enter Sarah Easton.

In 1891, she and husband Edward S. Easton — two of the city's most prominent citizens — built Easton Manor, a 11,000-square-foot mansion atop the Main Street hill. Edward Easton, whose fortune had come from the family grain business, organized the Peoria Board of Trade and served on the Peoria City Council.

After Edward Easton's death in 1901, his widow honored his memory by commissioning four fountains — each boldly etched "Easton" along Adams Street for the watering of horses, as well as any thirsty riders.

Easton Manor now hosts Converse Marketing. It sits next to Giant Oak Park, home to a massive burr oak tree on High Street. The park, operated by the Peoria Park District, also is home to one of three surviving Easton fountains.

The park district owns another Easton fountain, currently undergoing repair but soon to return to its spot at the Kinsey Memorial at Glen Oak Park. The other is privately owned yet displayed at Junction City. The fourth fountain is long gone.

101 THINGS THAT PLAY IN PEORIA

CLUE FOR NEXT ITEM: What time is it? You always know at this prodigious Pekin timepiece.

'World's Greatest Sundial' helps keep time in Pekin

PEKIN — When Henry Cakora started to build a sundial in the early 1990s, he had a lot of learning to do.

He hadn't much used sundials. But he wasn't clueless.

"I knew about the sun and how to track the sun," says Cakora, now 79. "And I'm good at mathematics."

Put that all together, and *voila* — his sudden inspiration that a sundial would be an interesting, classy addition to his hometown of Pekin. First, though, Cakora had to research celestial movement and measurements, calibrated by sundials for as many as 10,000 years. He learned about gnomons, analemmatic dials and other sundial parts,

101 THINGS THAT PLAY IN PEORIA

which he crafted at his family business, Tazewell Machine Parts. He talked to the Pekin Park District, which offered a chunk of land in the Sunken Gardens of Mineral Springs Park — south of Court Street, across the road from the lagoon.

There, volunteers helped put his dream together. There are actually three sundials, which tell time, dates, sun position and other facts. Plaques explain how to use the equipment, while a road sign proclaims, "World's Greatest Sundial."

The world's tallest sundial is known as Jantar Mantar, in India, which stands about 89 feet tall.

CLUE FOR NEXT ITEM: Left for dead in the Arbor District, it came back big — and heavy.

The tallest sundial in America is in Carefree, Ariz., stretching 62 feet.

So, at 45 feet tall, how is Pekin's the "greatest"?

"I'm sure, by far, it's the most accurate," Cakora says.

Rebecca Place arbor provides gateway to roots

The notion seemed unthinkable: the Arbor District losing its arbor.

Not just any arbor. The only arbor left in the city.

In 1912 and 1913, when the west edge of the West Bluff was Peoria's hot residential district, arbors were built in Bradley Park, along with each end of Rebecca Place: at Main Street and Bradley Avenue. Vines crawled up the columns and through the crossbeams, lending a stately touch to the neighborhood.

By 1973, only the Rebecca Place arbors remained, and both were crumbling. The city wanted to tear both down, but residents complained. In a nod to economics, the city ripped down the arbor at Bradley Avenue but repaired its twin at Main Street.

Not long into the 21st century, steel bands had been wrapped around the concrete columns to keep chunks from falling off. The city, worrying about concrete raining atop pedestrians and motorists, deemed the arbor a safety risk.

In 2006, the arbor came down. But the next year, a new one rose in its place.

The city spent $175,000 for a steel-reinforced concrete arbor, intended to last at least a century. Eight columns support two girders, each weighing four tons and topped with crossbeams.

It looks much like 1912 again — a very good year for the Arbor District.

101 THINGS THAT PLAY IN PEORIA

CLUE FOR NEXT ITEM:
With buttons, Peoria never forgets.

World contributed buttons to Peoria Holocaust Memorial

How can the mind comprehend the slaughter of 11 million people?

The Peoria Holocaust Memorial uses the simple visual image of buttons. Since 2003, 11 million buttons have stood at The Shoppes at Grand Prairie, commemorating the loss of 6 million Jews and 5 million others.

Launched in 2001, the project was coordinated by the Jewish Federation of Peoria. The organization picked buttons for several reasons, including their roundness as a representation of the circle of life. Furthermore, buttons were a part of clothes left behind at the gates of the concentration camps.

The two-year project involved the help of local schools, groups and volunteers who counted the buttons, which poured in from 49 states and five foreign countries. The buttons are encased in 18 glass columns in the shape of the Star of David. Eighteen is symbolic in Judaism for the word "chai," which means life.

Right now, because of exposure to the elements, the memorial is undergoing rehabilitation and cleaning. The memorial will be reinstalled later this year, though no date has been specified.

Israel, along with other nations, observes Yom HaShoah, or Holocaust Remembrance Day — which this year is April 16.

101 THINGS THAT PLAY IN PEORIA

CLUE FOR NEXT ITEM: For another Peoria memorial, his lyrics served as the perfect epitaphs.

A fitting tribute to Dan Fogelberg on Peoria riverfront

Memorials seem to come off as sad or drab.

Not the Dan Fogelberg Memorial. It's completely Fogelberg.

It's no mere marker. The commemoration simultaneously stands out and blends into Riverfront Park, a testament to the waterway Fogelberg loved.

Soon after the singer-songwriter died at age 56 in 2007, a band of friends and fans began soliciting donations for a tribute, with the City Council's blessing. Two years and more than $15,000 later, the group unveiled the memorial, centered by three large granite boulders. Each has lyrics from a Fogelberg song: "Part of the Plan" ("Love when you can, cry

when you have to"), "River of Souls" ("To every man the mystery sings a different song") and "Icarus Ascending ("Love is the only thing that matters").

A bench sits off a ways, marked with Fogelberg's photo, to allow visitors to take in a picturesque backdrop provided by towering trees and the flowing Illinois River. Along a trail heading to the memorial, smaller stones carry other Fogelberg lyrics, from "Ever On":

May the trail rise up to meet you

May your heart rejoice in song

May the skies be fair above you

As you journey ever on.

101 THINGS THAT PLAY IN PEORIA

CLUE FOR NEXT ITEM: Peoria hosts an honorary street for Fogelberg, but another — and funnier — native son has this actual street named after him.

Richard Pryor Place a stand-up tribute to comedian

Richard Pryor Place is not only a street but also a testament to Peoria's love-hate relationship with the comedian.

Onstage, the Peoria native gave a funny-scary glimpse into an urban world often ignored. For that, Comedy Central named him as the all-time greatest stand-up comedian.

But sometimes he used stark profanity and racial epithets, which many Peorians could not tolerate. Offstage, he made high-profile bad choices, almost killing himself, and Peoria didn't like that, either.

Still, in the 1990s, this newspaper beat the drum

to have a street named after Pryor. The City Council balked, waiting until 2001 — by the slimmest of margins, 6-5 — to grant Pryor a tiny slice of a street.

Without fanfare one day in October 2011, Public Works employees posted Pryor street signs along what formerly was Sheridan Road, from Romeo B. Garrett Avenue to McBean Street, plus one block of Persimmon Street. The total cost: $800.

Nice gesture? Perhaps. Then again, it's a section of town with relatively low traffic and visibility.

At the time, Pryor's manager said the comedian was

101 THINGS THAT PLAY IN PEORIA

"thrilled" by the gesture. Perhaps. But by then, multiple sclerosis had rendered him a recluse, so we never heard from Pryor directly.

He never returned to Peoria — to see the sign or anything or anyone else — before dying at age 65 in late 2005.

CLUE FOR NEXT ITEM: For baseball, their dance is corny.

Chiefs lend their ears to corny bit of good time

The Peoria Chiefs boast one of the corniest — and weirdest — rituals in all of minor-league baseball.

Whenever the team scores, two human-size ears of corn dance in the outfield. Makes no sense? Like many good stories, this recent tradition blends hard fact with a little baloney.

The corn first arrived in 2010, which — coincidence? — also marked the first season of the Normal CornBelters, who play in the independent Pioneer League. The Chiefs claim their dancing duo are named — coincidence? — "Norm and Al, our two corny friends from Normal."

According to the Chiefs,

"They were so excited the first time they saw the Chiefs score a run, they started to dance. Their wacky dance moves, to the tune of 'We Like to Party' by the Venga Boys, caught on, and they danced down a ramp, through the gates and right onto the center-field grass! The crowd went nuts, cheering them on, so Norm and Al continued to dance every time the Chiefs scored a run."

Usually, the corn couple simply bursts from behind the center-field wall after a run. However, they sometimes dance with props, including a limbo stick. Between innings, they occasionally can be seen shimmying to "YMCA" and dancing atop dugouts.

101 THINGS THAT PLAY IN PEORIA

CLUE FOR NEXT ITEM: This street without cars travels back to the West Bluff's yesteryear.

Closed to cars, it's also known as Lover's Lane

Moss Avenue hosts frequent behind-the-wheel sightseers eager to glimpse the expensive dwellings and expansive lawns.

But motor cars miss out on a quiet offshoot: Malvern Lane, a hidden sanctuary of red brick and colorful nature.

Malvern Lane was the first thoroughfare between the West Bluff and the valley below. It connected the rest of the city with what was mostly unsettled land when John Griswold built a home there in 1856. Today, the brick corridor spans Institute Place and Dr. Martin Luther King Jr. Drive.

Long ago, the road was known as "Lover's Lane" and rumored to bring good fortune and happiness to lovers who found the first wildflowers along the lane in the spring. Meantime, residents endured the incessant honking of cars traveling up and down the winding narrow lane, warning other cars of their presence and bugging the nearby homeowners

When the city of Peoria closed Malvern Lane to vehicle traffic in 1985, it also vacated ownership of the brick road to the property owners on either side. Westminster Presbyterian Church owns one side of the lane, while a group of private homeowners own the other.

Malvern Lane survives as a route for only cyclists and walkers, a meandering sliver of Peoria history that many locals have never seen.

101 THINGS THAT PLAY IN PEORIA

CLUE FOR NEXT ITEM: This tower stands above a castle that many Peorian's still reference by its old business name.

Jumer's a towering reminder to Bavarian memory

Peorians of a certain age can't help but think of 117 N. Western Ave. as anything but Jumer's Castle Lodge.

Sure, that spot hasn't been known by that name in more than a decade. In fact, it's no longer a hotel; it's an assisted-living center.

But if you've been around Peoria a while, a glimpse of the signature turret can't help but conjure wistful memories swirling with the likes of cinnamon rolls, the black bear and Jimmy Binkley.

The site long was home to Kramer's Drive-In, which James Jumer bought in 1960. A decade later, he envisioned a Bavarian theme, transforming the spot into the 168-room Jumer's Castle Lodge. It was known for elegance, to a large degree thanks to the antiques Jumer bought around the world and displayed in the inn.

Yet in 1999, Jumer's five-hotel chain (in Illinois and Iowa) filed for bankruptcy. Five years later, Jumer's was sold to a group that operated under the Radisson flag. James Jumer died in 2008, and the hotel folded a year later.

In 2011, after $7 million in renovations, the structure reopened as a 104-apartment facility called Courtyard Estates of Peoria. By then, interior mementos of Jumer's had been sold off, bought by souvenir-seekers eager to take home a piece of Peoria history.

But outside, the turret remains, still standing sentinel to Peoria's past. Its long, tall shadow reaches back to a time when success seemed to come easier — when it somehow made perfect sense to build a huge Bavarian castle to serve as a hotel in the middle of a residential area.

People came. And some still remember.

101 THINGS THAT PLAY IN PEORIA

CLUE FOR NEXT ITEM: This crumbled Downtown walk shouts shame, not fame — but still can be fixed.

Walk of Fame needs a little pep in its step

Maybe the Walk of Fame looks like a crumbled effort, but we prefer to see it as a work in progress.

It was a great idea when envisioned in 1994, in front of the Madison Theater. Tim Comfort, co-owner of the theater property, suggested the walk to Mike Sullivan, who was running the original S.O.P. pub, adjacent to the theater, at the corner of Madison Avenue and Main Street.

Sullivan launched the walk guerrilla-style: Act first, ask permission later. The city wasn't happy to discover Sullivan had uprooted a 3-by-3-foot slab of sidewalk and replaced it with a star for the late comedian Sam Kinison. Still, the city eventually warmed to the idea and gave Sullivan the go-ahead for two other inductees that year, opera star Jerry Hadley and sports announcer Jack Brickhouse.

But the project died as Sullivan moved on to other locales. The slabs for Hadley and Brickhouse survive, though Kinison's has inexplicably crumbled.

101 THINGS THAT PLAY IN PEORIA

Still, this year, a deal was announced to rehab the Madison Theater, plus build an adjacent mixed-use building of up to 14 stories. Surely, amid all the improvements, the Wall of Fame can't languish in its current sad state.

One option would be to rip out the stars and just pour cement. But that would be a shame. Instead, rekindle Sully's dream: Wrap the walk around the entire block. Let visitors stroll about and glimpse the names of luminaries produced by this town. Let's boast a little.

CLUE FOR NEXT ITEM:

Only a small marker notes a former airstrip.

Charles Lindbergh got Lucky after leaving Peoria

A plaque marks the site of the former airfield where Charles A. Lindbergh landed in Peoria on the St. Louis-to-Chicago mail run from 1926 to 1927, prior to his trans-Atlantic flight.

CLUE FOR NEXT ITEM:
Though the tractors and distillers long ago vanished into Peoria history, the outfield wall remains from their ballpark.

Before the world knew the daredevil pilot "Lucky Lindy," Peoria knew a mail carrier named "Slim."

On April 15, 1926, Peoria saw its first airmail, via a St. Louis to Chicago stopover. The pilot, a then-anonymous Charles Lindbergh, griped about the weather as soon as he landed: "It was bad all the way from St. Louis."

Lindbergh touched down at Peoria's first airport, Kellar Field (sometimes called Brown's Field, as it was located on the former Brown farm). That area is now the site of the High Point subdivision. There, along High Point road at High Point Lane, a tiny park sports a plaque noting, "Near this marker, Charles A. Lindbergh landed his DeHavilland Biplane on the St. Louis-Chicago mail run 1926 to 1927, prior to his trans-Atlantic flight."

That's mostly right, says Bob Keenan, historian/gardener at the Peoria airport. The owner of Kellar Field, Alexander Varney, opened a new airport in August 1926, then northwest of Peoria — a site now centered by Dick's Sporting Goods at The Shoppes at Grand Prairie. Most people called it Big Hollow Airport, though Varney simply referred to it as "Field No. 2." Regardless, Kellar Field shut down after the opening of the second field, which then became Lindbergh's landing point.

On May 22, 1927, newspapers worldwide carried headlines of a former airmail pilot who arrived in Paris — the first solo, nonstop trans-Atlantic flight.

Woodruff Field's left-field wall stretches back in time

L ike a blast over the outfield wall, the history of Peoria pro baseball goes way back — and a thick chunk of its yesteryear survives.

The city's first pro team, 1878's Peoria Reds, played at Lake View Park, at Adams and Grant streets. In 1923, with Lake View looking shabby, a better ballpark sprang up on the other side of Grant Street: Woodruff Field, built for a tidy $50,000.

That park, with a thick concrete block wall that surely spooked outfielders chasing long fly balls, served as home of the Three-I League's Peoria Distillers and Peoria Tractors, at different times between 1925 and 1935.

Despite a one-year re-vival in 1937, the field went dark professionally until 1953, when a rehabbed stadium hosted the Peoria Chiefs. In successive seasons, the affiliate was tied to the Cleveland Indians, St. Louis Cardinals and New York Yankees — though the biggest stars (such as Luis Aparacio and Roger Maris) tended to appear in the opposition dugout. Poor ticket sales ended pro ball at Woodruff Field after the 1957 season.

Minor league baseball would not return to Peoria until 1983, with the Peoria Suns at Meinen Field. Nineteen years later, at a new Downtown ballpark, the Peoria Chiefs won the Midwest League title, the first pro baseball title in Peoria since the '11 Distillers.

101 **THINGS THAT PLAY** IN **PEORIA**

Today, Woodruff Field survives, a nicely groomed spot for local youth and amateur programs. Beyond the diamond, the left-field walls remains, still stretching along Grant Street — and back in time.

CLUE FOR NEXT ITEM: Trains are an afterthought in Peoria nowadays, but this engine gets plenty of attention.

Storied steam locomotive 886 a reminder of railroading past

DUNLAP — The Rock Island Steam Locomotive 886 made the rounds before settling down at the Wheels O' Time Museum.

As the last steam locomotive to pull passenger cars into Peoria from Chicago, 886 has a prominent place in the area's transportation history.

Built by the American Locomotive Co. in Schenectady, N.Y., in 1910, the locomotive weighs about 126 tons. After retirement of the engine, former Caterpillar Inc. President Louis Neumiller and the Peoria Jaycees spearheaded a drive to display the locomotive in Peoria.

The train had several stops before finding a home at the museum. The Peoria Park District became the owner in 1956, displaying it at the lower entrance of Glen Oak Park. Later it was moved to Detweiller Golf Course. The Peoria Regional Museum Society became the owner when it was moved to Wheels O' Time Museum in 1985. In 2014, ownership was transferred to the Peoria Historical Society.

"The 886 locomotive is an attraction that all ages enjoy seeing," said museum spokeswoman Bobbie Rice. "The youngsters imagine what it must have been like to be an engineer and fireman. The children are fascinated by the sound of the whistle and the bell, while some of the adults can remember riding on a train pulled by a steam locomotive."

101 THINGS THAT PLAY IN PEORIA

CLUE FOR NEXT ITEM: No bull: At this longtime family business, the two biggest faces are bovine.

Big bulls help steer meat lovers to Alwan & Sons

Man's best friend might be a dog, but hereabouts, many meat lovers enjoy the company of bulls.

At least, that's the appearance at Alwan & Sons Meat Co., where two big bulls stand sentry outside the venerable butcher shop.

In 1947, brothers Oscar and Mason Alwan started Alwans Market in South Peoria. At one time, there were four like-named grocery stores. But in 1957, the main business — by then called Alwan Bros. — moved to Peoria Heights, taking over a former grocery store near the current location, 703 E. War Memorial Drive. Five years later, a new store was built there, and in 2006, the current structure went up. By then, the business had

101 THINGS THAT PLAY IN PEORIA

adopted the new name, Alwan & Sons Meat Co., now owned by a third generation: brothers Pat Alwan and Joe Alwan Jr., along with cousin Brian Alwan.

Along the way, the business moved away from groceries to focus on meat. In the late '50s, to underscore that difference, the shop brought aboard a key partner: a fiberglass black Angus bull. About 4 feet tall and 9 feet from nose to tail, it's about the size of the real thing.

The original bull remains out front of the store. But in 2006, after the new construction, the Alwan trio decided to bring in another bull, to catch motorists' eyes. That bull stands on an elevated stage on the side of the build-

CLUE FOR NEXT ITEM: The street name has changed, but whiskey barons built swanky homes here.

ing facing War Memorial Drive.

The bulls are about the same size. But the cost difference is remarkable. The first was bought for $20 at an auction. The second cost $8,000.

"It's crazy," Brian Alwan says with a laugh. "But there are only like two places in the country where you can get them. You can get a raggedy one for cheap, but it wouldn't be nearly as nice as the one we got."

77

High Wine gave them panorama of Peoria's growth

High Street is no mere road but a unique path to Peoria's past.

As the 20th century dawned, Peoria's economy was afloat in a river of whiskey. Peoria provided a confluence of plentiful ingredients: Midwestern grain, precise-temperature well water and low-cost coal. Distilleries popped up along the Illinois River, which at those times served as a perfect waste system.

The city quickly became the world's largest manufacturer of spirits, anchored by the world's largest distillery, Great Western (at the site of the present-day ADM plant). Still, the commercial boom came with costs, including harsh odors, frequent fires and severe injuries.

Of course, the whiskey barons did not want to live near this mess of industry. They, along with others who made fortunes from the industry, found an ideal spot on the West Bluff, where a lofty vantage allowed a wide scanning of a city largely being built on booze. Many mansions arose along the stretch of pavement they dubbed High Wine Avenue, employing a polite euphemism for whiskey. Homes include those built by the likes of Joseph B. Greenhut, Charles Corning and Edward Leisy.

Though the road's name long ago changed to the more inconspicuous High Street, much of the ornate 19th century architecture survives. Examples of Italianate, Flemish Renaissance, Second Empire and

CLUE FOR NEXT ITEM: No mere desks, these ancient rolltops have served as the stage of some of Peoria's finest political theater.

Queen Anne serve as a collective centerpiece for the High Wine Historic District.

Some of Peoria's greatest theater is around horseshoe

As a political stage, the Peoria City Council horseshoe has hosted dramas, comedies and everything in between.

As the centerpiece of council decision-making, the horseshoe always is influential, often disagreeable and occasionally comical.

At the fourth floor of City Hall, perhaps a chambers novice might see just a series of desks. The antique rolltops have sat in a semicircle since 1899, when City Hall opened.

At its core, the horseshoe plays a dutiful civic role. This is where Peoria moves forward or stagnates, where councilors hear or ignore pleas from the audience, where taxpayer money is spent this way or that.

It also has served as backdrop for some of Peoria's greatest theater. Recall the almost slapstick years when Mayor Bud Grieves often played ringmaster in trying to rein in a contentious and clownish council. Remember the absurdist moments of Councilman Gary Sandberg bringing along his pet macaw, Jelly Bean. And recollect the teary, inspirational scene of George Jacob returning to his council seat months after a debilitating injury to serve one final meeting, from his wheelchair.

The domelike council chambers recently underwent six months of renovations. During that time, the council hit the road, taking meetings to multiple sites, a nice breath of fresh air that brought city governance into various neighborhoods.

But the council is back home, setting the course of Peoria's future, from the familiar horseshoe.

101 THINGS THAT PLAY IN PEORIA

CLUE FOR NEXT ITEM: Way back when, he might not have been the biggest man on campus, but this big head marks his local legacy and global effect.

Reagan's legacy remains strong in Eureka

Eureka is proud of its connection to Ronald Reagan.

After graduating from Eureka College in 1932, Reagan gained fame as a movie actor before serving as a two-term president of the United States. But his presence remains strong in and around the school.

Banners across campus bear the Gipper's visage. There's also the Ronald Reagan Museum, the Ronald Reagan Peace Garden and the Reagan Physical Education Center. A few blocks from campus, the Reagan Trail wends its way across the state.

The centerpiece for all this adoration is the Reagan bust found in the peace

101 THINGS THAT PLAY IN PEORIA

garden. Sculpted by Peoria artist Lonnie Stewart, the bust sits atop a marble base inscribed with quotes from a speech Reagan delivered at the 1982 Eureka College commencement, announcing the goal for a strategic arms reduction treaty with the Soviet Union.

The peace garden, built with a gift from Peorians Anne and David Vaughn, also contains a large section of the Berlin Wall, a gift from the Federal Republic of Germany — and a reminder of Reagan's famous demand, "Tear down this wall!"

The campus also has graduated 42 college presidents, plus seven others

CLUE FOR NEXT ITEM: Bottled long ago, this freshwater now flows into Peoria's sewers.

who went on to become governors and members of Congress. None, of course, rose to the heights of Reagan, whose legacy was first shaped by Eureka College. Says college President J. David Arnold, "We celebrate what Eureka was able to do for Reagan."

Water that's fit for bottling at Peoria Mineral Springs

Of the "101 Things," Peoria Mineral Springs might be the most confounding.

The 14,000-year-old springs, once the city's main water supply, for generations now have been spilling — sparkling and cool, up to 30,000 gallons a day — into Peoria's sewer system.

Under the bluff rising from Martin Luther King Drive, a brick-and-mortar reservoir (which partially pokes out of the earth) dates back to the 1840s. The triple spring was operated as a major water supply until the early 1900s, when other sources were tapped. Meantime, water from the springs often was bottled and sold. R. Hickey Bottling Works sold Peach Cider and other beverages; later, Preston Clark marketed Peoria Mineral Spring Soda. But not long into the 20th century, the spring went dormant as a commercial interest.

In 1969, Charles Traynor bought the land, mostly as a place to raise his kids in the pre-Civil War home built there by the Moss family (now 701 W. Martin Luther King Jr. Drive). Still, Traynor sometimes dreamed of finding a way to do something with all of that water rushing from the springs.

Briefly, in 1980, Traynor sold the water to an Australian-based beverage company that made fruit juice. Other than that, the springs have kept bubbling unnoticed, right into the city sewers.

With health-conscious products in high demand,

CLUE FOR NEXT ITEM:
In this would-be municipality, Peoria kids learn to pedal properly.

the 76-year-old Traynor thinks the springs could be ripe for marketing. Still, for years he has been unable to spark much civic, commercial, historical or collegiate interest in the site.

He says the reservoir needs about $50,000 in repairs, but the water remains as fresh as ever.

"I've been all over the world," he says, "and the water here is wonderful. There's a lot of potential."

81

At the time, Bicycle Safety Town was revolutionary

Now a Peoria institution, Bicycle Safety Town arrived as cutting-edge idea borrowed from Europe.

The Sheridan Road course, where countless Peoria-area children have learned to ride bicycles, was the brainchild of late Peoria conservationist Bill Rutherford.

"It was one of the first bicycle safety towns in the U.S., and it was Bill Rutherford who brought the idea over to us from Europe," said Bonnie Noble, executive director of the Peoria Park District, the governmental unit that's run Safety Town since the mid-1970s.

It started in 1966 with the Forest Park Foundation, which ran a program called Council on Responsible Driving. Formal bicycle safety classes continue today, and the facility is popular with families who want to teach their children to learn the rules of the road.

The three acres of land now offers more than safe biking lanes and 79 traffic signs. Visitors will also find a family rest room, toddler-sized playground and picnic shelter.

Safety Town is also a familiar host for birthday parties. The cost is $25 per hour.

Otherwise, the park is free and open from dawn until dusk, seven days a week, closed only during bike-safety programs. Safety Town has one basic rule: Helmets are required for all who bike there.

For more information, call 694-5145.

CLUE FOR NEXT ITEM:
Start your engines:
For gearheads,
it's the sound
of summer.

82

Every summer, speedway roar rings out across West Peoria

For gear heads, it's the sound of summer: the rumbling thrum of automobile engines.

Locally, you'll hear it at Peoria Speedway, located outside of Peoria along Farmington Road.

Peoria Speedway opened in 1948 in what is now Pioneer Park and moved to its current location in 1965. The quarter-mile dirt track used to prompt frequent noise complaints, but a redesign of the oval has curbed the decibel levels.

That's not to call it quiet. Every warm-weather Saturday night, West Peoria resounds with the hum of engines in the distance.

The main enemy of the track: Mother Nature. Spring floods have wiped out scads of races; one even destroyed a massive chunk of grandstand.

Yet the track endures. Its slogan: "Stock car races, like old times." And roaring, just like old times.

CLUE FOR NEXT ITEM: At this outdoor venue, you won't watch cars — unless, perhaps, it's "A Streetcar Named Desire."

Corn Stock Theatre beats the heat with iconic tent

A local passion for summer performances birthed Corn Stock Theatre in 1954, but a fundamental problem loomed:

What about the heat?

At the time, few homes had air conditioning, nor did Peoria's theaters. The fear was, specta-

tors wouldn't pay to bake inside stifling venues during torrid months.

So, the new troupe decided to play outside. That summer, Corn Stock Theatre produced "Gigi" beneath a tent erected in Detweiller Park.

The location was nice, but nearby railroad tracks often caused unwanted show-stoppers. When ear-splitting trains rumbled by, actors literally had to stop in their tracks until the noise dwindled.

For the second season, the group moved to upper Bradley Park. The venue succeeded, though rain on the tent often sounded like the beating of a

CLUE FOR NEXT ITEM: This outdoor venue hosts bands— big ones in the '70s, as Stevie Nicks knows.

drum. In 2003, the group switched to a vinyl tent, which offers better acoustics.

Though mounted on a permanent frame, the vinyl tent is removable for the winter. Each spring, a crew of a half-dozen volunteers needs a day to get the tent and surroundings back into performance shape. When they're done, it's one of the most recognizable structures in Peoria.

It's durable, too. Despite wind, rain, heat and twisters, Corn Stock has canceled just two of about 2,700 shows over the past 60-plus years. That's quite a tent.

Amphitheater once hosted big-name music acts

It's hard to imagine Billy Joel or Stevie Nicks traipsing through Glen Oak Park.

But during a two-year run in the mid-'70s, Glen Oak Amphitheatre hosted pop music acts that these days could fill an arena.

Nowadays, the bandshell is perhaps best noted for its annual July 3rd fireworks display, as well as performances by the Peoria Municipal Band and other local groups. The park's original bandshell, constructed in 1896, was replaced by the current set-up in 1960. For more than a decade thereafter, big names were few there, unless you count Charlie Rich in '74.

But in 1976, before the debut of the Peoria Civic Center, rock promoter Jay Goldberg decided to try rock concerts at the amphitheater. The first show featured heavy sets by Nazareth and former Deep Purple frontman Ian Gillan, followed later that month by Jeff Beck opening for Fleetwood Mac ($7.50 per ticket). The other two shows that summer offered a softer sound, first with The Captain & Tennille, then The Beach Boys — the latter of which included opener Billy Joel, still a year from releasing "The Stranger."

In 1977 and 1979, Goldberg slated a handful of other shows. All sold well, but Goldberg was dogged by noise complaints.

"In that neighborhood,

the houses are so close," he says. "You won't believe who got the most complaints: The Beach Boys."

So, Goldberg moved on to other venues, and Glen Oak Park went back to more civic-minded affairs. These days, the annual fireworks are louder than The Beach Boys ever were, but no one complains.

101 THINGS THAT PLAY IN PEORIA

CLUE FOR NEXT ITEM: This old footbridge not only stretches back in time, but to another country.

85

Japanese Bridge a lasting testament to designer

Of all the local works designed by Frederic J. Klein, perhaps his most novel is the Japanese Bridge.

Born in Detroit in 1874, Klein was raised in Peoria. After an apprenticeship as an architect, he later would earn fame for designing homes and buildings elsewhere, including the elaborate Coronado Theater in Rockford.

But Klein left his biggest footprint in Peoria. His designs include the Madison Theater and the Apollo Theater, plus many stately homes. Klein helped develop Grandview Drive, and designed several residences there. In addition, he helped develop and lay out sections of Glen Oak Park, while the beautiful doors of the Springdale Cemetery Mausoleum also were of his design.

Especially with public designs, Klein strove for uniqueness. None of his theaters was similar in style, yet all reflected a sense of luxury and opulence, offering a glimpse at settings atypical to the workaday masses.

That description well suits his Japanese Bridge in lower Bradley Park. The footbridge, which spans Dry Run Creek, was constructed for $5,500 in 1922. The decorative open railing, along with the detailed portal, reflect Japanese-style architecture.

Klein died at Methodist Hospital in 1957. His Japanese Bridge, thanks to occasional rehab, survives as a singular Peoria attraction.

101 THINGS THAT PLAY IN PEORIA

CLUE FOR NEXT ITEM: If you want to see your name in lights, this marks the biggest, brightest spot in Peoria.

Peoria Players Theatre is known for longevity — and marquee

Peoria Players Theatre is the nation's fourth-longest consecutively running community theater — and

the longest in the state of Illinois. To no small degree, the big marquee has helped by drawing attention to three generations of shows.

"Our marquee is one of the last 'chasing lights' marquees in Peoria," says theater manager Nicki Haschke. "We continually try to nurse it along and keep up with the maintenance, as parts can be hard to find."

In a way, that's a good problem to have. It means you're a survivor.

Peoria Players Theatre grew out of a meeting held on June 25, 1919, when 35 people gathered at a home on Knoxville Avenue. The theater group performed for many years at the Peoria Women's Club, eventually settling into its current location at University and Lake in 1957.

Seven years later, the wide mar-

quee was added. It was built above the theater, designed by a Peoria Players member with a day job as an engineer. With repairs here and there, the marquee continues glowing as a bright theater beacon.

"Many times when (new) customers come to our shows, they may not know in which building we are located," Haschke says. "But the minute we mention the marquee, they immediately know where they are going.

"Our theatre building is located on one of the busiest intersections in the city and therefore serves as an excellent source of advertising."

CLUE FOR NEXT ITEM:
Sometimes called Prairie School, this pioneering architecture can be found at just one spot in Peoria.

Renowned Frank Lloyd Wright left mark on Peoria

By the turn of the 20th century, Frank Lloyd Wright had begun to assert himself as a creative architectural force, as Peoria would soon learn.

In 1888, the 19-year-old Wisconsin native went to work as a draftsman for Chicago architect Louis Sullivan, the "father of the skyscraper." Though Sullivan's firm focused on commercial works, Wright dabbled in residential design, eventually going out on his own.

He started designing his Prairie School dwellings, many around Chicago. The style involves extended, low structures blending with the flat, prairie landscape.

In 1903, Wright was commissioned to design a home at 1505 W. Moss Ave. by Francis W. Little, a lawyer and utility company owner. Little and his wife were founding members of the Art Institute of Chicago, and they owned a Wright home near Minneapolis. Though the couple lived at the address for less than a year, they left an enduring civic contribution: the only Wright design (by some still known as "The Little House") in Peoria.

The home features wide, overhanging eaves and reflects colors and texture from nature. The exterior planting areas near the

house are defined with low brick walls that add horizontal emphasis.

The residence is private, something to remember if you stop to take a glimpse. The home last sold in September 2008 for $559,000.

101 THINGS THAT PLAY IN PEORIA

CLUE FOR NEXT ITEM:
In an odd bit of irony, few Peorians have seen this original tool pioneered here for the visually impaired.

Peoria is the birthplace of red-tipped canes for the blind

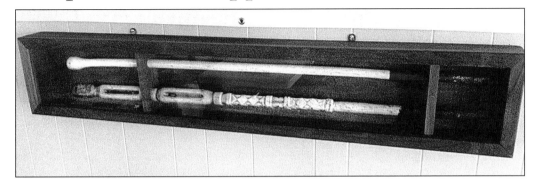

Of all "101 Things," today's perhaps suffers from the worst case of underexposure: Know it or not, Peoria is the birthplace of the red-tipped white walking cane, a universal symbol of the sightless.

In 1930, Elmer Thomason, a blind newspaper-stand operator in Peoria, had trouble crossing a busy intersection. A friend, George Bonham, noticed Thomason's dark wooden cane, wondering if perhaps a little innovation could aid Thomason's plight. Bonham, a member of the Peoria Lions Club, collaborated with Thomason to paint the cane white, then add a red tip — a way to catch the attention of motorists and others.

Peoria passed the nation's first white-cane ordinance, granting right-of-way to the visually impaired.

The Lions Club started producing the canes and giving them away to blind people, who suddenly found themselves with a measure of mobility and independence that many had not enjoyed before. Eventually, the Lions Club would distribute the canes to nearly 200 countries.

Today, the two original canes are on display at the Central Illinois Center for the Blind and Visually Impaired, 2905 W. Garden St. Perhaps at least one belongs in the Peoria Riverfront Museum to mark Peoria's pioneering role in advancing accessibility for the blind.

Meanwhile, much in the spirit of the white cane's originators, the center provides free white canes. The center — which this year celebrates its 60th anniversary — can be reached at 637-3693 or info@cicbvi.org.

CLUE FOR NEXT ITEM: This famous Peorian's final resting place is the site of what you might call a pink pilgrimage.

Komen marker has become touchstone for legions

Susan G. Komen means different things to different people.

To many, the name harks to the organization that has invested $1.5 billion in breast cancer care, education and research. The reference also conjures images of jogging shoes and heartfelt hugs at the yearly Race for the Cure. And the label applies to other fundrasing activities that help fund the group's efforts.

But for others, the most solemn connection to Susan G. Komen comes at her resting place.

Komen, a Peoria native, died of breast cancer in 1980 at the age of 36. In her name, sister Nancy Brinker launched a global movement that has become the world's largest source of not-for-profit funds dedicated to the fight against breast cancer.

Komen was laid to rest in a Parkview Cemetery vault. In 2009, a new Illinois Historical Society marker was placed near Komen's crypt, designating it a state historic landmark.

The spot has becoming a touchstone for legions of people connected to breast cancer. Before each year's May race, Komen family and staffers lay a wreath at the grave site in her honor. Each October, another wreath is placed there, to commemorate Komen's birthday, as well as Breast Cancer Awareness month.

Meanwhile, many survivors make special trips to the grave site. Often, out-of-town visitors stop at the local affiliate's office, eager to share stories about the strength and inspiration they glean from the legacy of Susan G. Komen — including a pilgrimage to her resting place.

101 THINGS THAT PLAY IN PEORIA

CLUE FOR NEXT ITEM:
Readers demanded this entry, as there's no better way to see Peoria than via this view.

Few vistas are as memorable as this one on I-74

Interstate travel is often mundane, with a local exception of the approach to Peoria from the east.

In one special place, you get the gift of drive-thru sightseeing.

West-bound on I-74 in Tazewell County, the four-laner wends gently around the East Peoria hillside. From that heightened vantage, just before the roadway gradually dips down the bluff and toward the Murray Baker Bridge, the view explodes, expansive and impressive along the west bank of the Illinois River.

Man's modern skyline stretches above and along nature's ancient waterway, reaching for the limitless sky.

Of all "101 Things," this view - this singular, sensational view — was the entry that readers demanded most. As one wrote, "It's magical at night. We would be returning from my grandparent's home when I was a kid, and when we would come around the bend, Peoria was sparkling there in the valley, like some Midwestern Oz."

It's hard to take a photo of such a thing. Sure, you can snap a quick shot. But the sight never seems as glorious as the one longtime locals carry in their mind, this impression — day or night — of our city at its resplendent finest.

CLUE FOR NEXT ITEM: Amid the burgeoning West Main Street commercial district, this space-age doodad beckons with retro flair.

Peoria has space to turn attention back to 1957

Sputnik 1 triggered the space race, then landed along American roadsides.

Not the actual Soviet satellite, of course. After sputniks first shot into orbit in 1957, a new-found U.S. fascination with space-age gadgetry brought replicas atop eateries, car lots and other high-traffic businesses. The blinking beacons lured customers suddenly enchanted with the melding of science fiction, deep space and international politics.

Now? They're a symbol of yesteryear's kitsch, much of which you can find on sale at Urban Artifacts, 925 N. Sheridan Road. The three-year-old shop traffics in art and antiques, heavily steeped in retro pop-culture — the likes of drinking glasses sporting '60s cartoons, light-up signs boasting long-defunct brands and letterman jackets touting shuttered schools.

101 THINGS THAT PLAY IN PEORIA

Yet, even before entering, you get the hint as to the way-back feel from a glimpse of the shop's signature signage: a rooftop sputnik near the front door. Owner Jon Walker, who bought the light-up satellite years ago but never knew its initial location, says the sputnik attracts attention from passersby — just as intended during the '50s and '60s.

"People notice it," he says. "It's like something you'd find way back when on Route 66."

CLUE FOR NEXT ITEM:
A sign of a different type, this one is big and grassy — and changes all the time, at the whim of weather and youths.

A sign of times: Price of land has fallen $1 million?

EAST PEORIA — The area's most noticeable billboard is made of grass.

Northeast of the McClugage Bridge, a wide hill rises up the bluff wedged between U.S. Route 24 and Illinois Route 116. For decades, that green background has hosted messages scrawled in white, often with toilet paper or plastic garbage bags. Some last for weeks, others only hours, washed away by rain.

The brief bulletins tend toward the innocuous, devoid of vulgarities. Still, many messages remain mysterious, their full meaning known only by the sender. Passers-by, with just a few moments' glimpse, try to decode the intent.

Some declarations are simple, perhaps a set of initials set below, "I LOVE." Other times, the message might be just a pair of initials within a heart: That could signify romantic love or hark to the loss of someone. Access is difficult, involving a steep uphill climb from the roadside. This is the handiwork of young people.

For years, the 80-acre parcel has been for sale, as noted by a sign near the top. The land is mostly zoned agricultural, with seven flat acres at the top zoned for residential or commercial development. The asking price: $600,000, or $1 million less than in 2009.

Even with the discount, that's quite a pricey billboard.

101 THINGS THAT PLAY IN PEORIA

CLUE FOR NEXT ITEM: Though located near many loud animals, these two big cats don't make a sound.

Stone lions at Peoria Zoo one of many Triebel legacies

The Peoria Zoo's oldest lions still are going strong after more than 130 years.

They don't need much food or care, either — thanks to Otto Triebel.

In 1853, the 23-year-old German sculptor arrived in Peoria. Otto Triebel and Sons, a successful dealer in stone, was contracted by the county to build a low stone wall around the courthouse in 1870.

Nine years later, Triebel decided to take a chance creatively and craft two stone lions. As he worked, he aimed to attract a specific buyer.

"Mr. Triebel intends to make them so handsome that the (County) Board of Supervisors will not be able to resist the temptation to buy them," according to the Peoria Daily Democrat.

His gambit succeeded, and the lions stretched along the Adams Street side of the courthouse for more than eight decades. But in 1963, the Peoria County Courthouse was razed, and the lions needed a new home.

The Peoria Park District came to the rescue and relocated the Triebel Lions to the zoo, where they have stood outside the front entrance for more than a half-century.

Triebel, a prominent citizen who served terms as city treasurer and county supervisor, gave Peoria another iconic creation: son Frederick Ernst "Fritz" Triebel, likely the city's greatest artist. The son's legacy includes the Soldiers and Sailors Monument in the Courthouse Plaza and the Robert Ingersoll statue in Glen Oak Park.

The Peoria Zoo stone lions were crafted by Otto Triebel in 1879 and have stood outside the zoo entrance for more than 50 years.

101 THINGS THAT PLAY IN PEORIA

CLUE FOR NEXT ITEM:
Mostly paved with bricks, this road dives like a roller coaster, with bumps that could leave you achin'.

Storied Aiken Avenue Peoria's own urban four-wheel slalom

Where San Francisco boasts Lombard Street, Peoria has Aiken Avenue.

Granted, the latter isn't quite the roller-coaster ride as the former, a West Coast motoring landmark with eight steep, hairpin turns. Still, if you're looking for cheap thrills, Aiken Avenue has its moments.

("Aiken Alley" had its moments, too — of infamy. It wasn't a real alley but a nickname for the stretch of Aiken Avenue that hosted numerous bawdy houses.)

The best way to launch onto Aiken Avenue is to motor east along Martin Luther King Drive, then hang a right onto Aiken. The turn is at an angle of about 60 degrees, which means you don't have to slow your speed as much as with a typical turn. Not that we advocate carelessness; we're just explaining automobile physics here. Plus, the road dips fast, meaning you could bottom out if you're not careful.

Careening along the steepness, you'll soon notice that the brick road slopes toward either side of the curbing. Stay as close to the middle of the road as possible.

Still, you'll encounter choppy brick, asphalt patching and periodic potholes, along with random rises and dips.

There are two ways to take on Aiken. You can grip the wheel hard and putter along slowly, which is the safest method. However, especially after a few practice trips, a driver can learn to navigate the challenges by giving the wheel plenty of play. Let your vehicle sort of meander itself, taking care not to plow into any potholes or anything else.

After a while, you'll get the hang of the four-wheel slalom — a unique Peoria sojourn, only on Aiken Avenue.

101 THINGS THAT PLAY IN PEORIA

PHIL LUCIANO/JOURNAL STAR

Aiken Avenue in Peoria features a brick road that slopes toward either side of the curbing, providing a choppy ride that's best taken at a slow pace.

CLUE FOR NEXT ITEM: This double-statue celebrates advice from an Illinois lawyer who admired drinking water in Tennessee.

A tribute to Lincoln's humanity outside Metamora Courthouse

Most tributes to Abraham Lincoln focus on grand accomplishments such as saving the union and ending slavery.

But a statue in front of the Metamora Courthouse captures a low-key moment of Lincoln's legal career that highlights his inherent humanity and decency.

In 1858, client Melissa Goings stood accused of killing her abusive husband, Roswell Goings. When he attacked her, she said, she struck him with a piece of firewood. The judge hearing her case seemed to be leaning against her, despite sympathies of townsfolk.

During a recess, Lincoln and Goings left the courtroom. Only he returned.

Queried as to her whereabouts, Lincoln denied explicitly aiding her escape but noted his client had said she was thirsty. Legend has built around his final words, re-

101 THINGS THAT PLAY IN PEORIA

putedly, "… and I said, Tennessee has mighty fine drinkin' water."

After she fled, the sheriff made no effort to track her down. A year later Lincoln persuaded the state's attorney to drop the charges.

To memorialize the event, the Woodford County Historical Society raised more than $100,000 for statues of Lincoln and Goings. The works, by John McClarey, were unveiled in 2009 in the town square, not far from the courthouse entrance.

The case merits a mention in the movie "Lincoln," starring Daniel Day-Lewis. The star namechecks Metamora during a recitation of the story, putting central Illinois onto the silver screen.

CLUE FOR NEXT ITEM: This outdoor flea market boasts a swank setting.

Moss Avenue sale combines trinkets, treasures, architecture

With its venerable mansions, spacious gardens and ornamental ironwork, Moss Avenue stands as one of the city's grandest - and most historic — thoroughfares.

It's also an upscale setting for a flea market, now known as the Moss Avenue Antique & Collectible Sale. The sale, in its 35th year, does more than provide an opportunity for browsers to pick up bric-a-brac: It's the sole source of income for the Moss-Bradley Residential Association.

Moss Avenue is closed to car traffic that day, but the Peoria County Sheriff's Office Posse patrols on horseback. Food vendors are a part of the mix, as is the convivial spirit between residents and visitors.

"Who eats onion rings at 9 in the morning? We do on Moss Avenue on the day of the sale," says Moss Avenue resident Dan Callahan. "Who leaves their front door unlocked for eight hours while total strangers walk by? We do — no problem."

It's free to peruse the merchandise. Callahan says a frugal day of entertainment can be had for $5: "That covers food and a doodad."

CLUE FOR NEXT ITEM: In Peoria, it's THE place for root beer.

One of the last places to get an old-fashioned root beer

Denise Graham pulled up to the counter at Lou's Drive-In on a hot summer day and explained her order: "Root beer out of a barrel. Seriously, who else does that?"

Lou LaHood bought the original barrel in 1949. He and his wife, Margaret, opened the outdoor restaurant at 4229 N. Knoxville in 1953, via a deal with Richardson

Root Beer. Richardson is long gone, but Lou's is going strong, having passed from Lou and Margaret to daughter Peggy Brown, who this spring sold the business to former employee Laurie Dean.

The constant for more than 60 years has been the root beer, brewed daily in a large vat with a precise mix of carbonated water, sugar and syrup; the recipe handwritten by Lou. After being hand-stirred with a wooden paddle, it's pumped out front to the wooden barrel, equipped with refrigeration coils that keep the root beer at 33 degrees. Each individual drink is tapped into a glass mug that's been chilled in a 45-degree water bath.

And no ice.

"It tastes different with ice or if it's put in the refrigerator," Brown says. "It's not as good."

The cold, creamy mix is the runaway favorite at the outdoor counter. A double batch, requiring 10 gallons of syrup, is made every morning. By comparison, Lou's goes through about five gallons of Coca-Cola

syrup in a week.

"I love it when people say it tastes the same as it did 50 years ago," Brown says. "They say it's exactly how they remember it."

CLUE FOR NEXT ITEM:
Quietly, this war weaponry has stood sentinel over Glen Oak Lagoon for more than a century.

Taking shot at preserving history for another century

Anchored to new moorings since 2014, Peoria's Spanish-American War booty is ready to face another century or more standing sentinel over Glen Oak Lagoon.

A cannon was brought back to the city as a prize after the 1898 conflict. It has been on display at the north end of the lagoon since 1899, for countless generations of children to clamber over, and for history buffs to squint at the Spanish inscriptions around it, including the name of the one-time 1,200-pound bronze weapon, "Arapiles."

The landmark spent much of the last dozen years on shaky ground after its parapet developed large cracks in 2002. Temporary repairs saw the whole structure blocked off from public access. Repair bids in ensuing years proved too costly to complete. Preservationists amped up a push for landmarking it due to its historical significance.

Then in 2014, a more cost-effective repair project fixed the decorative platform — and added handicapped accessibility. The final product incorporated the original stones from the wall at the edge of the lagoon. Now, the cannon rests on a granite housing after getting a professional cleaning and bronzing.

101 THINGS THAT PLAY IN PEORIA

CLUE FOR NEXT ITEM: This spot marks the resting spot of the lone Peorian — just one ... really ... even after all these years? — to hold the highest elected office in Illinois.

Springdale marker remembers only Peoria governor

Despite having been settled long before Illinois became a state, Peoria boasts a connection to only one governor in the nearly 200-year history of the Land of Lincoln.

Thomas Ford, the state's eighth governor and a Democrat, rests with his wife and one daughter underneath a large slab of stone in a quiet part of Springdale Cemetery along the side of Rose Hill.

He boasts some impressive accomplishments, one modern pols might envy. Faced with substantial state debt left from earlier infrastructure improvements, he worked throughout his single term to set the state on the path to fiscal solvency.

But Ford is mostly remembered for his role in the "Mormon Expulsion" of 1844. Tensions were running high between church leader Joseph Smith's followers and those who opposed the church in Nauvoo. Ford encouraged Smith to turn himself in to face charges of destroying the local newspaper, with either an implied or explicit guarantee of protection. Smith and his brother Hyrum were killed by anti-Mormon groups — a blot on the governor's record.

Some legends hold that Smith uttered some type of curse on Ford and his family. Regardless of the truth of those stories, the governor saw little luck after he left office. His wife died of cancer two years later at age 38. Ford, 50, followed her weeks later with tuberculosis. Two of his sons were killed decades later.

CLUE FOR NEXT ITEM:
Though gone since 2010,
he still looks over his last pub.

Iconic saloonkeeper still looking on benevolently

PEORIA HEIGHTS — It's comforting to know you still can walk into a Peoria pub and see Mike Sullivan.

Sully, Peoria's saloonkeeper extraordinaire, has been gone since 2010. Yet you still can see him on the wall of his last joint, Sullivan's — which for five years has been the Publik House, 4614 N. Prospect Road, Peoria Heights.

His roster of entertainment venues in and around Peoria included Sully's Beach Pub, Sully's Irish Pub, Sully's Pub & Cafe, Z.Z. Pop's, Texas Cafe, Khaki Jack's, S.O.P.'s and F. Scott's Whiskey Bar & Great Steaks. He had a gift of design, yet a better gift of gab. The shaggy-haired imp was always vocal, opinionated, tireless and assertive. A paratrooper during the Vietnam War, he loved a good fight, often using his bar as a pulpit to rail against City Hall.

Yet he always maintained a special Sully sense of serenity. At the end of a day, if you had time to spare, Sullivan made for a perfect companion. Lousy day? Sully would offer a goofy story to take off the edge. Great day? Sully would give you a hearty congrats, and probably a beer on the house.

That's why it's good to see him on the wall at the Publik House, clad in his black beret. His expression seems pensive, which belies his usual grin. Then again, his piercing gaze makes you wonder what's going on inside that playful Irish noggin, historically never an unusual feeling among those who knew him well.

The picture keeps us guessing and talking. In that way, as well as every time someone recalls another of the endless Sully anecdotes, he'll always be part of Peoria.

101 THINGS THAT PLAY IN PEORIA

A photo of Mike Sullivan hangs at the Publik House in Peoria Heights.

CLUE FOR NEXT ITEM: As a point — a very high point — of civic pride, this small-town mountain stands as a monument to mining days of yore.

Little village of Roanoke proud home of a jumbo attraction

With a jumbo, beauty is in the eye of the beholder.

The massive slag heaps dot the landscape as reminders of coal-mining heydays. Not everyone finds them pretty. But for the most part, folks see them as a point of nostalgia - and sometimes a very high point, as in hundreds of feet tall.

Mostly north of Peoria, coal companies sunk shafts into the earth in the late 19th century. While pulling out the precious coal, they had to do something with the byproducts — clay, shale, sulfur and coal waste — usually just piling it up, for decade after decade.

In many communities, the coal veins went empty in the early decades of the 20th century. When those companies left, towns struggled — though many survive today.

As for their jumbos, some were altered or eventually disappeared. For safety reasons, Mark's twin jumbos were pushed together, greatly flattened and shoved away from a nearby road. Minonk's vanished when used for fill to create overpasses for Interstate 39. Others — such as those in Toluca, Ladd and Wenona — remain as mountainous anomalies amid the flat croplands.

The village of Roanoke sports the jumbo nearest Peoria. Mining began there

101 THINGS THAT PLAY IN PEORIA

in 1881, lasting until 1940. The 100-foot-tall mound is known to many as Mount Jumbo, which many of the 2,000-some residents used to climb - on foot or bicycle — in their youth.

But no more. The jumbo, which is privately owned, has been closed for safety reasons. Still, the U.S. flag remains up top, a proud accent to the heaping source of civic pride.

CLUE FOR NEXT ITEM: Despite this fort monument, the Peoria area lacks much recognition for its French history.

Fort Crevecoeur monument a tribute to area's French origins

It's a winding journey to find the monument to Fort Crevecoeur, perhaps a fitting tribute to the exploring spirit of the founding Frenchmen.

And its relative obscurity also bespeaks a peculiarity about Peoria: Why is there so little recognition of its French heritage? You can glimpse a block-long LaSalle Street on the East Bluff, a marker at St. Mary's Cathedral honoring French missionaries and the Pere Marquette Hotel. But as for 150-plus years of French heritage, there's little else.

Across the river, you can visit the 89-acre Fort Crevecoeur site, including a simple yet solemn monument that has commemorated the fort since 1920. But that site was never definitively proven: Other possibilities include East Peoria (near Centennial Drive) and even Peoria (at the foot of Lafayette Street).

101 THINGS THAT PLAY IN PEORIA

Wherever it was, Fort Crevecoeur was founded in January 1680 — seven years after Louis Joliet and Jacques Marquette canoed into the river valley — by Robert Cavalier, Sieur de LaSalle, and Henri de Tonti. That April, the fort was burned and abandoned in favor of Fort St. Louis, at Starved Rock. Later, after interactions there with Indians left Tonti with a stab wound, he returned downriver, where in 1691 he established a fort known by various names, including Fort Pimiteoui — the site of modern Peoria. It was the first European settlement in Illinois and one of the earliest in the middle of America.

The area long served as an important trading post. The French flag flew until 1863, when it was replaced by Britain's Union Jack. But as far as Peoria is concerned today, it sometimes seems as if the French banner hardly flew here at all.

CLUE FOR NEXT ITEM: This marker stands on land, but memorializes a waterway wreck.

Pekin marker notes steamboat Columbia tragedy

On July 5, 1918, the South Side Social Club of Pekin sponsored an Illinois River excursion by the sternwheeler Columbia. At 7:30 p.m., the steamboat picked up passengers in Kingston Mines before stopping in Pekin for more fares, heading upriver at 8:15 with 496 people — men, women, children — aboard. The boat churned to Al Fresco Park, north of Peoria, stopping for 30 minutes before turning around for the return trip.

North of Wesley City (now Creve Coeur), with the river shrouded in dense fog, a submerged tree stump tore a gaping hole — 11 feet long and 2 feet wide — in the hull. The boat sank into 16 feet of water, with passengers struggling to stay afloat amid the shrieking chaos and make it to the shore. One was Lucille Adcock, 18, of Pekin, who clung to a flagpole to stay alive; the last survivor of the wreck, she died at age 106 in 2006.

Eighty-seven passengers died, including 57 people from Pekin. The dead were brought to the Pekin riverfront for identification.

That spot now hosts the Columbia Riverboat State Historical Marker, a grim but fitting reminder of one of the nation's worst inland maritime disasters.

101 THINGS THAT PLAY IN PEORIA

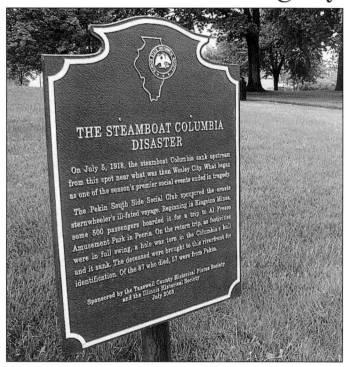

THE STEAMBOAT COLUMBIA DISASTER

On July 5, 1918, the steamboat Columbia sank upstream from this spot near what was then Wesley City. What began as one of the season's premier social events ended in tragedy.

The Pekin South Side Social Club sponsored the ornate sternwheeler's ill-fated voyage. Beginning in Kingston Mines, some 500 passengers boarded it for a trip to Al Fresco Amusement Park in Peoria. On the return trip, as festivities were in full swing, a hole was torn in the Columbia's hull and it sank. The deceased were brought to this riverfront for identification. Of the 87 who died, 57 were from Pekin.

Sponsored by the Tazewell County Historical Places Society and the Illinois Historical Society
July 2003

CLUE FOR NEXT ITEM: It's the last working reminder of Peoria's distillery past.

Still fermenting a lot of history along distillery row

In the mid-19th Century, Almiran Cole heated a batch of corn in his new kettles, fermenting not only Peoria's commercial spirits but the start of an industry that would transform the town into The Whiskey Capital of the World.

Cole, a Massachusetts native and Peoria merchant, began his distillery at the current site of the Cedar Street Bridge. Others followed his lead. By 1865, Peoria boasted 14 distilleries strung along the Illinois River, from what is now the State Street Post Office to Interstate 474 at Bartonville. By 1880, at the height of production, Peoria pumped out a world-high 18.5 million gallons of spirits.

Distilleries couldn't find a better match of resources: plentiful grains, pure spring water, available coal and wood fuel, handy rail and river transportation — and, the Illinois River, then a convenient dumping ground for waste. Plus, the distilleries created jobs for coopers, tinsmiths, wagon drivers and other professions.

101 THINGS THAT PLAY IN PEORIA

CLUE FOR NEXT ITEM: For veterans (or anyone) on Memorial Day (or any day), you'd have a hard time finding a bigger Old Glory than this one.

Hiram Walker & Sons, a Canadian distillery, began operating in Peoria in 1934. By 1959, the distillery was producing 127,000 gallons of bourbon whiskey per day and employed 1,150 workers.

But by the 1970s, the nation's tastes had turned from hard liquor to wine and beer. The company shuttered the business in 1979, the end to the last distillery in Peoria.

In 1982, Archer Daniels Midland took over the plant, which now churns out ethanol. ADM ferments grain — much like Almiran Cole.

105

Patriotism on display at Veteran's Pub & Pizza

CLUE FOR NEXT ITEM: This South Peoria steel sculpture serves as a bridge — and stands near a small one — between African-American influence and modern Peoria.

For a prodigious presentation of patriotism, you can count on a veteran — in particular, Veteran's Pub & Pizza.

A super-size Stars and Stripes hangs outside, on the north side of 2525 NE Adams St., a tavern known for its support of military causes and fundraisers.

Owner Darrell Amerman used to display an even bigger banner, stretching 16 feet by 20 feet, on the southern exterior wall.

"Normally, a flag that big will be displayed at corporations or big business buildings," says Amerman, commander of the Military Order of the Purple Heart, Chapter 175.

But last year, that south wall became part of a new beer garden. With no room there anymore for the big flag, the garden's roof instead is topped with a slew of military and veterans flags.

On the opposite side of the pub, the other oversized Old Glory greets the endless parade of motorists heading toward Downtown, a constant reminder of the red, white and blue.

"That's how people know this place, by that flag," Amerman says.

101 THINGS THAT PLAY IN PEORIA

Sculpture honors NAACP

The walking-path entrance to John H. Gwynn Park is an appropriate site for an African-inspired steel sculpture.

The 15-foot-high artwork stands in a grassy space just off MacArthur Highway, between entrances to Valley Park Shopping Plaza and Valeska Hinton Early Childhood Development.

It was the first, and so far only, public sculpture commissioned by the local chapter of the NAACP, the organization Gwynn served for more than 30 years.

Originally located in a neighborhood park across from the old NAACP office along what was then Second Street, the sculpture was uprooted and moved when the NAACP office moved, then moved again to the current location.

Sculptor Allen "Uzikee" Nelson, a former Peorian now based in Washington, D.C., created the work — his first — in 1970.

He says his work is meant to rejuvenate memory. Nelson didn't name it, but NAACP members called it "Doc," in part to memorialize his father, the late dentist Dr. John Nelson.

But it also commemorates the NAACP, along with the African-American influence that helped shape his father and Peoria.

Acknowledgements

The staff of the Journal Star contributed to this book for 101 consecutive days in February, March, April and May, 2015, and included:

Pam Adams, Jennifer Adler, Dennis Anderson, Mike Bailey, Joe Bates, Thomas Bruch, Matt Buedel, Johnny Campos, Kevin Capie, Shannon Countryman, Matt Dayhoff, Adam Duvall, Dave Eminian, Brad Erickson, Katie Gaston, Adam Gerik, Chris Grimm, Teressa Hargrove, Scott Hilyard, Scott Hinton, Wes Huett, Josh Jenke, John Komosa, Ron Johnson, Chris Kaergard, Andy Kravetz, Andy Latora, Phil Luciano, Brian Ludwig, Sally McKee, Stan Morris, Dean Muellerleile, Laura Nightengale, Michael Noel, Merry Rebholz, Leslie Renken, David Reynolds, Robert Ryan, Kathy Rynearson, Anthony Smith, Rachel Smith, Amanda Stoll, Lonnie Schwindenhammer, Steve Tarter, Troy Taylor, Nick Vlahos, Kirk Wessler, Mickey Wieland, David Zalaznik and Fred Zwicky.

We greatly acknowledge the efforts of Columnist Phil Luciano, Senior Web Producer Matt Dayhoff, Assistant Universal Desk Editor-Days Chris Grimm, and the photography department, including Assistant Managing Editor-Digital Adam Gerik, Visual Assignment Editor Fred Zwicky, Photographers Ron Johnson and David Zalaznik and News Assistant for Photos and Graphics Teressa Hargrove.

The 101 Things That Play In Peoria logo was created by Graphics Editor Michael Noel.

47571846R00062

Made in the USA
Lexington, KY
09 December 2015